Eilat & the Negev

Vanessa Betts

Credits

Footprint credits
Editor: Felicity Laughton
Production and layout: Emma Bryers
Maps: Kevin Feeney

Managing Director: Andy Riddle
Commercial Director: Patrick Dawson
Publisher: Alan Murphy
Publishing Managers: Felicity Laughton,
Jo Williams, Nicola Gibbs
Marketing and Partnerships Director:
Liz Harper
Marketing Executive: Liz Eyles
Trade Product Manager: Diane McEntee
Account Managers: Paul Bew, Tania Ross
Advertising: Renu Sibal, Elizabeth Taylor
Trade Product Co-ordinator: Kirsty Holmes

Photography credits
Front cover: Gorshkov13/Dreamstime.com
Back cover: kavram/Shutterstock.com

Printed in Great Britain by CPI Antony Rowe,
Chippenham, Wiltshire

Publishing information
Footprint *Focus Eilat & the Negev*
1st edition
© Footprint Handbooks Ltd
October 2012

ISBN: 978 1 908206 89 3
CIP DATA: A catalogue record for this book
is available from the British Library

® Footprint Handbooks and the Footprint
mark are a registered trademark of
Footprint Handbooks Ltd

Published by Footprint
6 Riverside Court
Lower Bristol Road
Bath BA2 3DZ, UK
T +44 (0)1225 469141
F +44 (0)1225 469461
footprinttravelguides.com

Distributed in the USA by Globe Pequot
Press, Guilford, Connecticut

The content of Footprint *Focus Eilat &
the Negev* has been taken directly from
Footprint's *Israel Handbook* which was
researched and written by Vanessa Betts
and Dave Winter.

Contents

LEBANON

Mt Hermon

Kiryat
Shemona

SYRIA

Nahariya

Akko   Safed

Haifa   Tiberias
                        Sea of
                        Galilee

Mediterranean
Sea

Nazareth
            Afula
Megiddo   Bet
Caesarea   Shean   Jordan River
            Jenin   Border Crossing

Netanya   Tulkarm
            Qalqilya   Nablus
Herzliya
TEL AVIV/   WEST
JAFFA   BANK

Ramla   Ramallah   Allenby/
Rehevot   King Hussein
            Jericho   Bridge
Ashdod   Jerusalem   *Qumran*

            Bethlehem
Ashqelon
            Hebron   *Dead*
                        Sea
Gaza City
            'En Gedi

Rafah   Be'er Sheva *Masada*
                        Arad

EGYPT   Dimona   JORDAN

            Mizpe
            Ramon

            Eilat   Arava Crossing
            Taba   Aqaba
                    Gulf of
                    Aqaba

N

20 km
20 miles

4 • Eilat & the Negev

There is far more to the Negev than just the hedonistic beach resort of Eilat stuck on the bottom of a large stretch of desert. This is an area to explore in depth, rather than view through the window of a bus en route from Tel Aviv. If the option is available to you, this is the place to hire a car (or camel), and visit the superbly preserved remains of the Nabatean-Roman-Byzantine cities at Avdat, Mamshit and Shivta. The Negev is also a physically beautiful environment, no more so than at Ein Avdat National Park, where the contrast between icy blue pools of water and dry, brown barren hills is brought sharply into focus. Meanwhile, at the very heart of the Negev is a spectacular natural geological phenomenon: the Makhtesh Ramon erosion crater is the place to get your hiking boots on and your 'Every Boy's Guide to Rocks and Minerals' out of your luggage. And finally, there is Eilat, Israel's premier resort.

The Dead Sea is a stunning, almost shockingly beautiful region, where white salt and desert sands meet the still blue waters of the hazy lake. It is also the setting for Masada, a site whose archaeological importance is matched by its visual impact: panoramic views from the mountain-top location and Herodian remains that bring the past alive. This is a site in Israel that no-one should miss. The Dead Sea Region also contains Qumran, the place where the famous (and controversial) Dead Sea Scrolls were discovered. Further south, you can hike through idyllic Ein Gedi Nature Reserve, while the less chartered wadis and mountains of Sodom are easily accessed from the friendly moshav of Ne'ot HaKikar, right on the border with Jordan. And then of course there is the Dead Sea itself. Fighting for survival, with the water receding year by year, the lowest point on earth still calls people to experience its therapeutic and cosmetic benefits as it has done for millennia. Even if you don't avail yourself of a treatment in one of the numerous spas, make time to float in the salty waters – a most peculiar sensation.

Planning your trip

Best time to visit Eilat and the Negev

Climate

The climatic seasons in Israel are the same as those in Europe (and the northern hemisphere). Thus spring is roughly March to May, summer is June to August, autumn (fall) is September and October and winter is November to February. As a very general guide, winter tends to be rather wet and overcast, becoming colder and wetter the further north or the higher up you go. The Dead Sea Region and the Negev are particularly appealing at this time of year, with very comfortable daytime temperatures. Indeed, winter is an ideal time to take a beach holiday in Eilat.

Climatic conditions in spring are ideal across most of the country, notably in the Negev and Dead Sea Region, where daytime temperatures have not climbed too high. At the height of summer, however, the Dead Sea Region and the Negev can get far too hot to be comfortable. As summer turns to autumn around September, the entire country becomes an attractive proposition, with comfortable temperatures and little rainfall.

Holidays

Unless you are coming to Israel specifically to celebrate a religious holiday (whether Jewish or Christian), the main holiday periods are best avoided. Flights to and from Israel just before or after religious holidays tend to be heavily booked, and you will almost certainly end up paying more for your ticket. Likewise, accommodation prices rocket (sometimes double), and in some places it can be difficult to find a room without an advance reservation.

The key Christian festivals are of course Easter and Christmas, though the accommodation shortfalls and problems of overcrowding at major sites only really affect visitors to Jerusalem and Bethlehem. Note, however, that different branches of the Church celebrate these events at different times, and hence the Christmas and Easter rush can become quite an extended period.

Jewish holidays and festivals are numerous, though the key ones are Rosh Hashanah, Yom Kippur, Sukkot and Pesach. Though the holidays are generally brief (usually one day), you should bear in mind that the holiday affects all aspects of life in Israel. Not only do accommodation prices sky-rocket, but almost everything else closes down (including places to eat, sights, banks, post offices and transport). When several holidays come along together it can have a major impact on your visit. Dates of Jewish holidays follow the lunar calendar and thus change each year, though the approximate time of year remains the same. Thus, September/October may be a time to avoid since Rosh Hashanah, Yom Kippur and Sukkot all come along together. Likewise, April/May tends to feature Pesach, Independence Day and Holocaust Memorial Day. For full details of holidays and festivals see the section starting on page 16.

Getting to Eilat and the Negev

Air

The majority of visitors to Israel arrive by air. Most arrivals are at **Ben-Gurion Airport** (at Lod, some 22 km southeast of Tel Aviv), though some charter flights land at **'Uvda Airport**

(60 km north of Eilat). Ben-Gurion Airport can get very crowded during holidays when it can take almost an hour to clear immigration on arrival. For further details on Ben-Gurion Airport, including getting there and away, see below.

At peak periods not only do air fares rise dramatically, but it can also be difficult getting a flight in or out of Israel. Such peak periods include the time around Jewish and Christian holidays, plus the peak periods associated with school holidays in the country of the flight's origin. You are advised to book tickets for these periods well in advance.

Ben-Gurion Airport For general 24-hour airport information call T03-9755555 or *6663, or see www.iaa.gov.il. Recorded information for departures/arrivals/transportation, T03-9723332, in English, 24 hours. All international flights arrive at Terminal 3, and the vast majority also depart from there, save for a couple of low-cost airlines which check in at Terminal 1. Domestic flights also depart/arrive from the old Terminal 1.

To/from the airport Trains and are the only form of public transport to/from Tel Aviv (buses leave from outside the airport grounds, connected by airport shuttle bus). The train service operates 24 hours. From Hagana train station in Tel Aviv it is a short walk to the Central Bus Station, from where buses leave for Eilat.

Sheruts (24 hours) are the only means of public transport to/from Jerusalem, leaving from outside the arrivals hall (Nesher, T03-9759555, one hour). Taxis are in abundance outside the arrivals hall.

Arrival formalities You can ask the immigration staff at passport control not to stamp your passport if you want to avoid an Israeli stamp. This leaves you with no printed record of your entry date. This generally only poses a problem at border crossings (to the West Bank, Egypt, Jordan), when Israeli security officials might ask where your stamp is. A phone call to an authority figure follows, and then you will be allowed to pass. Do not mention any travel plans to the West Bank if questioned on arrival at Ben-Gurion, as this will only arouse suspicion.

Departure formalities Ensure that you arrive no less than three hours before your flight departs. Be prepared for thorough questioning by the security staff before you check in (which can be lengthy). Bear in mind that this is done for your own safety. On exiting passport control, if you avoided an Israeli stamp when you arrived you can avoid getting one now, but only if you ask.

For obvious reasons, airline security on planes flying in and out of Israel is probably the tightest in the world. Whether you are flying in or out of Israel, you should check-in at least three hours prior to departure. El Al also use their own airline security staff abroad.

Prior to checking-in at Ben-Gurion or 'Uvda Airport to board a flight out of Israel, you will be questioned thoroughly by the airline security service. How long this cross-examination lasts depends upon a number of factors: your name and ethnic background, the stamps in your passport, your appearance, and where in Israel you admit to having been.

Airport facilities There are limitless opportunities for frenzied duty-free shopping upon arrival or departure. There is free Wi-Fi throughout Terminal 3. All the major car-hire firms have offices at the airport, most of which are open 24 hours. A number of companies offer mobile phone hire. Banks here do not offer the best deals: change just enough to tide you over until you can go to more competitive places in Tel Aviv or Jerusalem. VAT refunds are processed at the **Bank Leumi** in the Departures lounge. There's a post office and shopping area (including **Steimatzky** bookshop, cafés, restaurants) before exiting through passport control. Baggage storage facilities, T03-9754436, are found at the short-term car park, ground level, Sunday-Thursday 0800-1945, Friday 0800-1430, 20NIS per 24 hours.

Road
Israel has land borders with Lebanon, Syria, Jordan and Egypt, though currently it is only possible to cross overland into the latter two. Information on all the border crossings can be found at www.iaa.gov.il.

To/from Jordan Jordanian visas can be obtained upon entry at most of Jordan's air, sea and land entry/exit points, though visitors arriving at the Allenby/King Hussein Bridge crossing from Israel will not be given visas on arrival. For further notes on travelling in the region, see box, page 9. Fees vary according to nationality. Visas issued at point of entry are valid for a period of two weeks, but can be easily extended in Amman. Alternatively, you can apply to the Jordanian Embassy in your own country. Security procedures for entering Israel from Jordan are very strict and it may take some time to cross the border. Israeli immigration will stamp entry-exit stamps on a separate piece of paper if you so request.

Yitzah Rabin/Arava Crossing This is located about 4 km north of Eilat on the Israeli side and 10 km northwest of Aqaba on the Jordanian side. From Eilat it can be reached by taxi (30NIS) or by bus (get dropped by the Eilot turning from where it's 1.5 km walk); see 'Transport' in the 'Eilat' section on page 89. The border is open Sunday-Thursday 0700-2200, Friday-Saturday 0800-2000, closed on Yom Kippur and Jordanian holidays. For details on crossing the border from the Israeli side, T08-6300555. If leaving Israel, a departure tax of 98.5NIS must be paid. Jordanian visas are available on the border and a Jordanian entry stamp will appear in your passport. If leaving Jordan, a JD departure tax must be paid and a Jordanian exit stamp will be entered in your passport. There are currency exchange facilities on both sides of the border.

Allenby/King Hussein Bridge Closest to Jerusalem (16 km east of Jericho), there are special regulations in force at this crossing point. Leaving Israel, the departure tax is 163NIS (since both Israel and the Palestinian Authority collect a share). Jordanian visas are not available on the border, you must arrange them in advance. The Jordanian entry stamp will not be entered on your passport, but on a separate piece of paper. If you also leave Jordan through this crossing point, the only evidence of your visit to Jordan will be a visa (but no entry/exit stamps). If you leave Jordan through any other exit, you will get a Jordanian exit stamp in your passport. From the crossing point there are buses and taxis to Amman. Leaving Jordan, a JD departure tax must be paid. There are currency exchange facilities on both sides of the border. The crossing is open Sunday to Thursday 0800-2330, Friday and Saturday 0800-1300, closed on Yom Kippur and Jordanian holidays, though aim to cross as early in the day as possible. Note that you cannot walk across the bridge (but have to pay an extortionate amount for a five-minute bus ride). Israelis are not permitted to cross at this border.

To/from Egypt Rafah crossing: This border crossing is closed to travellers indefinitely, so all overland travellers to Egypt go through Eilat/Taba at present.

Eilat/Taba crossing: Tourists who intend visiting Sinai only need a 14-day Sinai permit, which is issued at the border crossing. Those wishing to travel beyond Sinai require a full tourist visa which must be arranged in advance in Tel Aviv or Eilat. It is easiest and

The entry-exit stamp game

Anybody intending to travel beyond Israel into Arab and/or Muslim countries may like to avoid having Israeli entry and exit stamps in their passport. Fortunately, Israeli immigration officials are quite happy to assist here and will, on request, stamp a separate sheet of paper rather than your passport. This is fine if you fly in or out of Israel, though if you leave or arrive by land it is difficult to avoid an Egyptian or Jordanian entry-exit stamp. An entry stamp that says that you arrived in Egypt at Taba, for example, means that you can only have come from one place – Israel. In the wider world this is no great hassle, though it will almost certainly prevent you from ever using the same passport to get a Syrian, Lebanese or Sudanese visa (amongst others). Even entering Jordan through the Allenby/King Hussein Bridge, where the Jordanian entry stamp is given on a separate piece of paper, does not appear to help matters. The Syrians will scan your passport for a Jordanian entry stamp, with the lack of one (presuming you've hidden the piece of paper) telling the Syrians where you have come from.

It helps to get such visas as far in advance as possible, preferably in your home country. Note that it is difficult to get a Syrian visa in Jordan, even if you have never been to Israel. If you do have Israeli or Israel-Jordan/Israel-Egypt entry/exit stamps, getting a new passport is one solution, though again, the Syrians, Lebanese and Sudanese are suspicious of new passports issued at embassies in Cairo and Amman. The easiest solution is to plan your trip carefully so that you visit Lebanon and Syria before Israel.

quickest in Eilat at **visa services** ⓘ 68 Efroni, T08-6376882, in an unassuming villa west of Eilat centre, Sun-Thu 0900-1430, but get there by 1400, visas (single or multiple) cost from 65-110NIS (depending on nationality), 1 x passport photo required. The procedure takes half a day. The Eilat/Taba crossing is open 24 hours a day. For details on reaching the crossing point from the Israeli side, see page 88). The Taba bus station is less than 1-km walk from the border, on the left after the Moevenpick Hotel. Buses to Cairo leave at 1030 and 1430 (60LE), and for Sharm el-Sheikh/Suez at 1500. Mini-bus taxis also wait immediately after the border crossing. To Cairo they cost US$100 (or 80LE per person if all 14 seats are taken); these are also useful for getting to destinations in Sinai if the bus times don't suit. Leaving Israel, you have to pay 98.5NIS departure tax, followed by 75LE Egyptian entry tax (paid on the bus at a checkpoint five minutes after leaving Taba bus station). You do not have to pay these taxes if you are just visiting the Taba Hilton casino. Leaving Egypt there is a 2LE departure tax (unless you have overstayed your visa which then costs 153LE). There are money-changers on both sides of the border, though rates to buy Egyptian LE are slightly better on the Egyptian side. Security procedures for entering Israel from Egypt are not particularly strict, but it still may take some time to cross the border. Israeli immigration will stamp entry-exit stamps on a separate piece of paper if you so request. For further details on the Israeli side, T08-6360999.

Departure tax

Departure tax for foreigners flying out of Israel is incorporated in the ticket price, but leaving Israel for Egypt by land, foreigners must pay 98.5NIS departure tax at the Eilat/Taba crossing. Leaving Israel for Jordan by land, foreigners pay 98.5NIS departure tax at the Jordan Valley and Arava crossings, and 163NIS at the Allenby/King Hussein Bridge.

Transport in Eilat and the Negev

Air

For visitors focussing on the Negev and Dead Sea, it makes sense to fly from Tel Aviv to Eilat, despite the compact size of Israel. The domestic airline **Arkia** have flights connecting Eilat with Tel Aviv's two airports (Ben-Gurion and the small Sde Dov airport north of the city center). For booking see www.arkia.co.il or call T09-8633480. **El Al** and **Israir** also fly to Eilat, with highly competitive prices (as low as US$15 one way). See www.elal.co.il and www.israirairlines.com.

Rail

Israel State Railways run a limited passenger network, but for travel between Tel Aviv and Beér Shevah. Many trains are express, meaning travel time is as short as one hour. Trains run as far south as Dimona. Fares are comparable with the bus service, though slightly more, and those with a student card get 10% discount, making it even more attractive. See www.rail.co.il.

Road

Bicycle Negev is a challenging region to explore by bicycle, and some careful planning is required. El Al does not charge extra for bringing a bike, see www.elal.com for details. The climate is a major consideration, notably high daytime temperatures in summer, especially in the Negev and Dead Sea Region. Make an early start, rest up during the hottest part of the day, and carry and consume plenty of water. Most roads (particularly the main highways) have wide hard shoulders so you should be able to remain safe. It may also be possible to put your bicycle on a bus for longer/difficult journeys (at 50% of the passenger fare). Look for bicycle itineraries on www.goisrael.com, and the **Israeli Cycling Federation**, www.ofanaim.org.il. Both Mizpe Ramon and Midrashet Sde Boker are renowned centres for biking trails and have expert shops/rental places.

Bus The **Egged Bus Company** provides the back-bone of the Israeli transport system, linking not just the major towns and cities but also all the remote villages, kibbutzim and moshavs. Because of the small size of the country, the longest journey you will conceivably undertake is six hours (Eilat to Haifa), and costs remain reasonable (under 80NIS for the longest journey). As a very general rule, Egged services operate from around 0530 until about 2230 Monday-Thursday. **Note** Remember that on Friday and on the eve of Jewish holidays, services stop at around 1500 and don't resume until sunset on Saturday. Plan your journey carefully if travelling at these times. Relying on the bus in the Negev and Dead Sea Region also requires careful planning since services are less regular.

Efficient bus information can be obtained by dialling *2800, and then pressing '9' or '0' to bypass the recorded message to a human voice. Keep requests simple – to/from, price, travel time – and you should have no problems. The helpful website, www.egged.co.il, takes a little getting used to but you will soon be familiar with it. Eilat is the only destination to which you can book advance tickets online. The information kiosks at the main bus stations have a very poor reputation for service, but often there is a free-phone booth in the bus station where an operator can provide you with immediate and accurate information. Large electronic boards give full details of all departures, including next and last bus and platform number. If travelling to remote areas, double-check bus times.

Intra-city services around town are operated by **Egged**, though other companies also operate local services. **Metropoline** (T5900*) operate around Be'er Shevam/Mizpe Ramon.

Be warned: urban bus drivers will shut the doors and pull away as soon as everyone is deemed to be on board. The driver will then collect the fares and give change whilst weaving through the traffic.

Car hire Hiring a car in Israel makes a lot of sense, particularly for exploring the Negev where public transport connections are poor. When divided between two, three or four passengers, a hire car can be excellent value. All the major international rental agencies are represented in Israel, along with a number of local firms.

It pays to shop around; ask about insurance and mileage charges before you commit. As a very general rule of thumb, the cheapest cars cost about US$30 per day including insurance. You only generally get unlimited mileage if you hire for three days or more. Check exactly what the insurance covers. Depending upon what time of year you visit, and where you intend going, think very seriously about getting a car with a/c. Most rental agencies require drivers to be over 21, though this rule is sometimes waived. You will require a clean (-ish) licence (international licence not generally necessary) and a credit card. You have to keep your passport, driving licence and rental agreement with you at all times when driving in Israel. It is usually possible to drive the car one-way and drop it off in a different city from where you rented it. Rental cars cannot be taken into Sinai (Egypt) or Jordan.

Israeli traffic drives on the right-hand side of the road. It is compulsory for the driver and all passengers to wear seat belts. Children under 14 must be seated in the back seat, and those under four must be strapped in to a suitable car seat. Urban speed limit is 50 kph (31 mph), and 90 kph (56 mph) on inter-city roads. On main arterial roads (eg Routes 1 and 4) 100 kph (62 mph) is permitted. It is compulsory in Israel to drive with headlights on at all times from 1 November to 31 March. Most traffic signs are self-explanatory, or similar to those used in Europe and North America. Other road regulations are similar. When in doubt, give way.

Regarding parking, where the kerb is painted red and white, parking and stopping is prohibited at any time. A blue-and-white painted kerb indicates parking permitted with a parking card (available from kiosks, post offices, etc) or by feeding a meter. Parking may be limited to one hour 0700-1700, though a sign should indicate this. Red-and-yellow painted kerbs are for buses and taxis only. Whenever possible, use a designated car park. Do not drive the wrong way in or out of a car park: the car trap will wreck your tyres.

Hitching Hitchhiking (*tremping*) remains a popular way of getting around Israel, especially in the Negev where bus services are infrequent. As with any other country in the world, there are inherent risks attached. A number of measures can be taken to reduce these risks, such as never hitching alone and being selective about whom you get into a car with. It is strongly recommended that women should never hitch without male company. To hitch a ride point down to the road with your index finger (don't use the 'thumb' system used elsewhere).

Taxi Taxis that operate around towns are metered, though fares are not particularly cheap. Taxi drivers are obliged to use their meters, so insist upon it, and even ask the name of the company and the driver if you suspect they might be 'trying it on'. Taxis can add a surcharge for a call out, for baggage, and may add 25% for night (2100-0530) and Shabbat services. It is possible to organize a 'special', whether for a tour around a particular town or a visit to a remote site that is poorly served by public transport. Be certain what the exact deal is (eg waiting time, etc), otherwise you are likely to be ripped off. Hotel and hostel receptionists, or the tourist office, may be able to give you some idea of what the fare should be.

Where to stay in Eilat and the Negev → *For hotel price codes, see page 13.*

Hotels

Israel has a very broad range of hotels and, as a general rule, the **$$$$** category hotels live up to their price tag, with facilities and service to match their 'luxury' pricing. Things can be a little more variable in the lower categories, with many of the hotels here holding themselves in too high esteem. If you are looking to stay in the 'top end' accommodation, it may be worth noting that the suites in some hotels offer very good value.

There are a number of considerations to bear in mind when booking/checking in to a hotel in Israel. Firstly, there is a huge variation in room charges according to the season. 'High' season generally coincides with Jewish and Christian religious festivals, and can see prices increase by between 25 and 50%. Note that the weekend (Friday-Saturday) is usually considered 'high' season.

Despite this blatant rip-off, in some places (notably Eilat and Jerusalem) it can be hard to find a bed during the 'high' season. Most of the rest of the year is designated 'regular' season, with a couple of weeks of 'low' season when tourist bookings are slack. The classifications in this Focus guide are for the 'regular' season. Note that the prices used here are spot/rack rates: if you book as a group or through a travel agency, you may be getting a significant discount. With all hotel classifications, look out for hidden taxes. An Israeli breakfast is included within the price at many hotels.

Remember that by paying in a foreign hard currency you avoid paying VAT. High-end hotel prices are almost always quoted in US dollars, and this is the preferred means of payment. Many hotels have specific characteristics that reflect the Jewish nature of Israel, such as in-house synagogues, Shabbat elevators (that stop at every floor and don't require buttons to be pressed) and kosher restaurants.

Note All accommodation in Israel (from five-star hotels down to backpacker hostels) is required by law to provide a free safe for depositing valuables.

Kibbutz guesthouses

Kibbutz guesthouses are an attractive option in the Negev, often located in isolated environs. They tend to be peaceful and quiet, well run, and with full access to kibbutz facilities such as swimming pools and private beaches, children's entertainment and restaurant/dining hall. A down side is that few are served by regular public transport.

Hostels

Hostels provide the cheapest accommodation in Eilat at around US$18-20 for dormitories. There is a big jump in price for double rooms, with the cheapest generally US$45-50. Some hostels give discounts for longer stays. Standards are variable. Dorm sizes vary between three and 30 beds, with some being single-sex and others mixed. Some hostels pride themselves on their 'party atmosphere', the idea being that they act as a meeting place for backpackers who want to go out and get drunk together.

A more than welcome addition to the hostelling scene is the **ILH organization**. This independent group of hostels/guesthouses has enrolled members whose beds are guaranteed to be clean, with a mix of dorm and private rooms, who nearly always provide kitchen facilities, have prices that are very fair and are in locations that are always interesting (eg in wood cabins, country kibbutzim or camel ranches). ILH hostels accommodate a range of budgets, are suitable for all ages, and are a good place to meet like-minded travellers, see www.hostels-israel.com.

Price codes

Where to stay

$$$$ over US$200	$$$ US$100-199
$$ US$30-99	$ under US$30

Prices include taxes and service charge, but not meals. They are based on a double room, except in the $ range, where prices are almost always per person.

Restaurants

$$$ over US$30 $$ US$15-30 $ under US$15

Prices refer to the cost of a two-course meal for one person, excluding drinks or service charge.

You don't need to be a 'youth' to stay at any of Israel's Hostelling International (HI) hostels; in fact most have a number of family rooms. In some of the more remote places of interest, **IYHA** hostels provide the cheapest (or only) accommodation at about US$30 per night. Without exception, they are spotlessly clean, offering a choice of spacious air-conditioned dormitories (usually single-sex); family rooms, sleeping four to eight people, air conditioned; and private rooms; all with en suite shower. Sheets and blankets are provided. Breakfast is almost always included, and evening meals tend to be generous and reasonable value (but only available if enough people are staying). Bookings are recommended during holidays and weekends, though these hostels can get very noisy with kids at these times. For further details see www.iyha.org.il.

The **Society for the Protection of Nature in Israel** (SPNI) operates Field Schools in this region, many of which have accommodation similar to IYHA hostels, though they are usually more basic, see www.aspni.org.

Camping

There are a number of fully equipped campsites in the Negev, though they are only really for those who are dedicated to sleeping under canvas. Camping in a hostel grounds is cheaper than sleeping in a dorm and may be a good compromise. You can generally camp for free on Eilat's southern beaches, though theft and security remain major risks. When trekking for a few days, 'wild' camping is an acceptable option (though of course you have to carry all your gear and camping equipment).

Private homes

Accommodation in private homes is available in Eilat and the Negev. You can respond to advertisements in the paper, notes on the wall in hostels, or signs hung outside homes for rent, though it is recommended that you make enquiries through the local tourist office (who should have a list of licensed places). Daily rates vary from US$40-60 per person, though weekly and monthly deals can be struck. Make sure that you see the place before handing over any money, and be sure that the deal is clear (eg heating, blankets, breakfast, etc).

Food and drink in Eilat and the Negev → For restaurant price codes, see page 13.

Despite a common bond (Judaism) Israelis have a diverse cultural and ethnic background. Not surprisingly, therefore, the dining experience reflects this diversity. Dining out can, however, be an expensive business. The cheapest eating options are provided by the ubiquitous falafel and *shwarma* stands, though eating at these three times a day is neither good for your health nor morale. Expect to spend US$20-25 a day for one decent meal plus two 'street meals' (less – if you don't eat meat, and stick to falafel and pizza). Hostels with their own kitchens can reduce your food bill.

Israel is (for those with a bit of money) a gastronomic paradise. Everyone you meet will recommend the best place in town to eat, and they usually know what they are talking about. Yes, it costs money, but the size of portion and the quality of the meal is way above what many visitors are used to. Diners in Israel can choose from a global menu, with Argentinean, Mexican, Italian, French, Chinese, Southeast Asian and Indian restaurants in the main cities. In many cases, the owners/chefs have strong links to the country that their restaurant claims to represent.

The staple of many Arab restaurants is barbecued meat on skewers (*shashlik*), *shwarma* (known elsewhere as doner kebab) and grilled chicken. Accompaniments include salad, falafel, hummus, bread, and possibly chips (fries), though put together these side dishes can provide a filling meal. One of the most delicious (and cheap) meals served in Israel is *fuul*: a plate of mashed fava beans served in garlic-flavoured oil with hummus and bread. More specialist dishes include *mansaaf*, usually a whole leg of lamb served on a bed of rice with nuts and lemon juice. A diet-busting Arab sweet dish, is *kanafeh*, a mild cheese mixed with pistachios and baked in a honey syrup shell.

Budget eating
It is possible to eat on a budget in Israel, though it is very easy to fall into a predictable diet of nutritionally poor food. The backpacker staple, considered to be Israel's national dish, is the falafel. This comprises ground-up chickpeas blended with herbs and spices, rolled into balls and then deep fried. They are usually served stuffed into a pitta bread with *tahini* (a thin paste made from sesame seeds) and salad. Such a sandwich costs 6NIS for a half and about 10NIS for a full sandwich, or even 15NIS (depending upon where you buy it). At many such streetside stalls you do the salad-stuffing yourself. A variation of this is the *shwarma* (see above), where the falafel balls are substituted by a form of processed lamb or turkey cut from a revolving spit.

Traditional Jewish
Some dishes associated with the Ashkenazi, or Eastern European, Jewish immigrants include good old-fashioned Hungarian goulash, Viennese schnitzel, chicken livers and gefilte fish. Perhaps more appealing are the Sephardi/Mizrachi, or 'Oriental', restaurants that are becoming more and more popular. Food here reflects the Sephardi roots in the Middle East, with many dishes such as the grilled meats and chicken being very similar to those found in Arab restaurants. Goose livers, baked sinia and stuffed vegetables are all specialities. Falafel (see above) and hummus (a thick paste made from ground chickpeas, garlic, seasoning and tahini) are also served as side dishes.

Kosher

The eating habits of observant Jews are governed by the *kashrut* dietary laws laid down by God to Moses (*kosher* being the noun of *kashrut*). Given the standards of hygiene likely to have been practised at this time, many of them make good sense, particularly in the area of prevention of cross-contamination. Many people are familiar with the *kosher* prohibitions against eating pork and serving meat and dairy products at the same meal, though there is far more to the *kashrut* laws than just this.

Beasts that are clovenfooted and chew the cud can be eaten (*Leviticus 11:1-47*; *Deuteronomy 14:6-7*). Hence you can eat a cow, which fulfils this criteria, but not a camel (since it chews the cud but is not cleft-hooved). Conversely pigs, despite being clovenfooted, do not chew the cud and so are forbidden. Only birds that do not eat carrion can be considered 'clean', whilst fish must have fins and scales; thus shellfish are forbidden (*Deuteronomy 14:8-19*). However, to be considered *kosher*, animals have to be killed instantly and according to methods supervised by the religious authorities. Animals that have died of disease, or in pain, are not considered *kosher*.

A *kosher* kitchen, whether in a restaurant or private home, will keep separate plates and dishes for cooking and serving meat and dairy products and will not serve the two together (*Exodus 23:19*; *Deuteronomy 14:14-21*). Such have been the culinary habits developed by Israelis over the years, however, you will not simply be given a black coffee to finish off your meal – a milk substitute will be provided. It is permitted for *kosher* restaurants serving dairy products also to serve fish.

Visitors should note that some restaurants are closed on Shabbat, though - bar a few extreme cases – finding somewhere to eat should not be a problem. Note that a restaurant that offers a *kosher* menu will not be given a *kashrut* certificate if it prepares or serves food on Shabbat.

Despite the strict regulations regarding *kashrut* dietary laws, few visitors to Israel will be inconvenienced by them, whilst the dining experience of vegetarians will be positively enhanced.

Vegetarian

Vegetarians, though not necessarily vegans, are pretty well catered for in Israel, usually as a by-product of the kashrut dietary laws. In addition to the chain of 'dairy' restaurants that can be found across Israel, a number of notable restaurants are preparing imaginative vegetarian dishes. In less cosmopolitan areas vegetarians may have to fall back on the tried and tested falafel and hummus formula, though many hotels prepare good-value eat-all-you-want breakfast salads.

Drink

You pay around US$5-7 for a beer in a regular bar, though these prices can be almost halved if you look out for happy hours and backpacker-oriented bars.

It is still said that Israelis are not big drinkers, though the recent massive influx of Eastern Europeans into the country appears to have replaced one stereotype with another. The most popular locally produced beers are Goldstar (4.7%) and Maccabee (4.9%), the latter of which is considered marginally better. Locally brewed-under-licence Carlsberg, Tuborg and Heineken are readily available at similar prices. A half-litre glass in a regular bar will cost 18-22NIS, or 10-12NIS if you drink in one of the bars catering to the backpacker crowd.

The German-style Ramallah-brewed Taybeh beer wins a lot of friends, though is not widely available outside of the West Bank.

A number of very good wines are produced in Israel, with notable labels coming from the Golan Heights Winery of Katzrin, the Carmel Wine Cellars in Zichron Ya'akov and the Carmel Winery in Rishon LeTzion. Imported wines tend to be expensive. A variety of spirits and fortified wines are also produced locally, with Israeli vodka renowned for its, er, cheapness.

Drinking coffee is a popular Israeli habit, with a wealth of cafés to choose from. Coffee served in Arab cafés tends to be the thick, bitter Turkish-style drink, complete with half a cup of sludge. Bedouin tea is strong and comes with desert herbs added. It is served in tiny glasses with generous amounts of sugar. Carbonated drinks are readily available. Expect to pay 6NIS for a can of Coke, while bottled water costs 4-5NIS for a litre (less in a big supermarket).

Festivals in Eilat and the Negev

Holidays and religious festivals in Israel present a very confusing picture. Not only are there 'secular', Jewish, Christian and Islamic holidays, but the dates that they fall on are variously governed by the Hebrew lunar calendar, the solar Gregorian calendar, plus sightings of the new moon at Mecca!

Jewish holidays

Israel works on the lunar Hebrew calendar (as opposed to the solar Gregorian calendar), and thus all Jewish religious and secular holidays fall on different dates of the Gregorian calendar each year. However, they always remain at roughly the same time of year. Most of the main Jewish holidays fall within the autumn season. Transport, banks, offices, shops and restaurants are all affected, whilst accommodation can be difficult to find in spite of the sky-rocketing prices. If you are here for one of the major holidays (Rosh Hashanah, Yom Kippur, Sukkot, Pesach), plan ahead. For details of the Jewish Sabbath (Shabbat) see under Opening hours, page 21. Dates are given here for 2013 and 2014. The holidays below are listed in the order in which they occur during the Hebrew calendar year, and not in order of importance.

Sep Rosh Hashanah Rosh Hashanah celebrates the beginning of the Hebrew calendar year. Because it is the only holiday in Israel that lasts for 2 consecutive days, it is considered to be the main vacation period. It is celebrated on the 1st and 2nd of Tishri. 2013: 4-6 Sep; 2014: 24-26 Sep.

Sep/Oct Yom Kippur This is the holiest day of the year and the most important date in the Hebrew calendar. It marks the end of 10 days of penitence and moral introspection that began with Rosh Hashanah, and finishes with God's judgement and forgiveness: the Day of Atonement. Virtually everything in Israel closes down for Yom Kippur and the roads are totally empty. It takes place on the 10th of Tishri. 2013: 14 Sep; 2014: 4 Oct.

Sukkot Sukkot commemorates the 40 years spent wandering in the wilderness after the Moses-led Exodus out of bondage in Egypt. Many Jews recreate the succah, or moveable shelter, in which the Israelites lived during their wanderings, taking all their meals there for a period of 7 days. It takes place on the 15th to 21st of Tishri. 2013: 19-25 Sep; 2014: 8-15 Oct.

Simchat Torah This is probably the only Jewish religious holiday in Israel that has no accompanying Zionist tradition. It celebrates the giving of the Torah (first 5 books of the Bible: *Genesis, Exodus, Leviticus, Numbers, Deuteronomy*); literally the Rejoicing of the Law. It falls 1 week after Sukkot, at the end of Tishri. 2013: 27 Sep; 2014: 17 Oct.

Months of the Hebrew calendar

Tishrey (Sep/Oct); Cheshvan (Oct/Nov); Kislev (Nov/Dec); Tevet (Dec/Jan); Shvat (Jan/Feb); Adar (Feb/Mar, Adar bet in a leap year); Nisan (Mar/Apr); Iyar (Apr/May); Sivan (May/Jun); Tamuz (Jun/Jul); Av (Jul/Aug); Elul (Aug/Sep).

Nov/Dec Hanukkah Not an official public holiday, since it does not mark an event mentioned in the Torah, Hanukkah celebrates the Maccabean Revolt that began in the 2nd century BCE when the Jews rose up against the pagan reforms of the dominant Hellenistic culture. The revolt culminated in a return to Jewish self-rule under the Hasmonean dynasty (c.152-37 BCE). Hanukkah is celebrated by the nightly ceremonial lighting of the menorah, or 7-branched candelabra, and is thus often known as the Feast or Festival of Lights. It falls during Kislev. 2013: 28 Nov-5 Dec; 2014: 16-24 Dec.

Jan Tu B'Shevat This is not a public holiday, though in recent years it has been used as an occasion for tree-planting. Its origins are in the Mishnah, when the 'New Year for Trees' was celebrated by eating fruit and nuts. 2013: 26 Jan; 2014: 16 Jan.

Feb/Mar Purim Purim is probably the most bizarre holiday in the Hebrew calendar. It celebrates events in ancient Persia when the Jews were sentenced to death for refusing to bow to the secular authority. For some reason Purim, or the Feast of Lots, has been turned into a sort of Jewish Halloween, with children dressing up and adults encouraged to get uncharacteristically drunk. 2013: 24 Feb; 2014: 16 Mar.

Mar/Apr Pesach Pesach, or Passover, celebrates the Exodus out of Egypt. The festival lasts for a whole week and, even though only the first and last days are official public holidays, many shops (including food stores) close for the entire 7 days. Pesach is celebrated from the 15th to 21st of Nisan. 2013: 25 Mar-2 Apr; 2014: 14-22 Apr.

Apr/May Lag B'Omer Lag B'Omer is really a multiple celebration. Taking place on the 18th of Iyar, it marks the end of a 33-day period of mourning and represents a sort of rite of spring when a plague was lifted from the Jewish nation. Bonfires are lit country wide. 2013: 28 Apr; 2014: 18 May.

May/Jun Shavuot In its original form, Shavuot commemorated the 7 weeks that it took the Israelites to reach Mt Sinai, and is thus something of a celebration of the receiving of the Torah. Under the Zionist influence of the early kibbutzniks, however, Shavuot has come to represent something of a celebration of the productive capability of the land, and is often referred to as the 'kibbutz holiday'. It takes place on the 6th of Sivan. 2013: 15-16 May; 2014: 4-5 Jun.

Israeli 'secular' holidays

Apr/May Yom HaSho'ah (Holocaust Memorial) Since 1951, the 27th of Nisan has been set aside as a day to remember both the victims of the Holocaust and the heroes of the Jewish resistance. Its official title is in fact Memorial to the Holocaust and the Heroism. 2013: 7 Apr; 2014: 6 May.

Apr/May Yom Ha'Atzmaut (Independence Day) David Ben-Gurion declared Israel's independence on 14 May 1948. Or rather he declared it on the 5th day of the month of Iyar. 2013: 16 Apr; 2014: 6 May.

May Day May Day reflects the socialist leanings of the early Zionists, though International Labour Day is now only celebrated on some kibbutzim (1 May).

Muslim holidays

The Islamic calendar The Islamic calendar begins on 16 July 622 AD, the date of the Hijra ('flight' or 'migration') of the Prophet

Mohammad from Mecca to Medina in modern Saudi Arabia, which is denoted 1 AH (Anno Hegirae or year of the Hegira). The Islamic or Hijri calendar is lunar rather than solar, each year having 354 or 355 days, meaning that annual festivals do not occur on the same day each year according to the Gregorian calendar.

The 12 lunar months of the Islamic calendar, alternating between 29 and 30 days, are; *Muharram, Safar, Rabi-ul-Awwal, Rabi-ul-Sani, Jumada-ul-Awwal, Jumada-ul-Sani, Rajab, Shaban, Ramadan, Shawwal, Ziquad* and *Zilhaj*. To convert a date in the Hijra calendar to the Christian date, express the former in years and decimals of a year, multiply by 0.970225, add 621.54 and the total will correspond exactly with the Christian year!

Ras as-Sana/Al-Hijra (Islamic New Year) 1st *Muharram*. The first 10 days of the year are regarded as holy, especially the 10th.

Moulid an-Nabi Birth of the Prophet Mohammad: 12th *Rabi-ul-Awwal*.

Leilat al-Meiraj Ascension of Mohammad from the Haram al-Sharif in Jerusalem: 27th *Rajab*.

Ramadan The holiest Islamic month, when Muslims observe a complete fast during daylight hours. Businesses and Muslim sites operate on reduced hours during Ramadan. 21st *Ramadan is the Shab-e-Qadr* or 'Night of Prayer'.

Eid el-Fitr Literally 'the small feast'. 3 days of celebrations, beginning 1st *Shawwal*, to mark the end of Ramadan.

Eid el-Adha Literally 'the great feast' or 'feast of the sacrifice'. 4 days beginning on 10th *Zilhaj*. The principal Islamic festival, commemorating Abraham's sacrifice of his son Ismail, and coinciding with the pilgrimage to Mecca. Marked by the sacrifice of a sheep, by feasting and by donations to the poor.

Essentials A-Z

Accident and emergency
Medical emergency: T101 (Hebrew) or T911 (English). A special medical helpline for tourists can be reached on T177-0229110. **Police**: T100. **Fire**: T102.

Conduct
Visitors (both men and women) should be prepared to dress conservatively when visiting Bedouin areas, ultra-orthodox Jewish neighbourhoods, and religious and holy sites of any creed. When visiting mosques, remember to remove shoes before entering. Women are generally permitted entry, though they should cover their heads. In synagogues, both men and women are required to cover heads. Public displays of affection at any religious site should be completely avoided.

Electricity
220 volts, 50 cycle AC. Plugs are of the round 2-pin variety. Adapters can be bought, though they are probably cheaper in your home country.

Embassies and consulates
For a full list of all foreign embassies and consulates in Israel, and Israeli embassies abroad, go to www.embassy.goabroad.com.

Health
See your GP or travel clinic at least 6 weeks before departure for general advice on travel risks and vaccinations. Make sure you have sufficient medical travel insurance, get a dental check, know your own blood group and, if you suffer a long-term condition such as diabetes or epilepsy, obtain a Medic Alert bracelet/necklace (www.medicalert. co.uk). Also, get advice from your doctor and carry sufficient medication to last the full duration of your trip. You may want to ask your doctor for a letter explaining your condition. If you wear glasses, take a copy of your prescription.

Travellers should consider carrying a small first-aid kit that contains such basic items as headache treatments (eg Paracetamol), preparatory treatments for diarrhoea such as Loperamide (eg Imodium, Arret), oral rehydration proprietary preparations (ORS), plus sticky plasters and corn plasters (eg Band Aid). A good insect repellent may also come in handy, particularly those with around a 40-50% concentration of Diethyl-toluamide (DET). There are also repellents available that use more natural ingredients. All of these items are available in Israel, though you will probably find that they are cheaper at home.

Vaccinations
Confirm your primary courses and boosters are up to date. It is advisable to vaccinate against diphtheria, tetanus, poliomyelitis, hepatitis A and typhoid. Other vaccinations that may be advised are hepatitis B and rabies.

Health risks
The standard of healthcare in Israel is very high (it leads the world in some fields). There are no special health precautions that visitors should take, except to avoid **dehydration** and **sunburn/stroke**. A wide-brimmed hat plus high-factor sun-cream should be worn as protection against the sun, whilst 4 litres of water should be drunk per day to avoid dehydration. Dark-coloured urine, perhaps coupled with a feeling of lethargy, is often a sign of dehydration. Tap water in Israel is safe. Bottled water is widely available. Sunglasses with 100% UV protection are a must. Note that not all clothes offer protection against the sun. As a general rule of thumb, if you can see through it when you hold it up to the light, then you can burn through it.

If swimming or diving in an area where there are poisonous fish such as stone or scorpion fish (also called by a variety of local names), sea urchins on rocky coasts, or coral, tread carefully or wear plimsolls. The **sting** of such fish is intensely painful but can be helped by immersing the stung part in water as hot as you can bear for as long as it remains painful. This is not always very practical and you must take care not to scald yourself. It is highly recommended that you take immediate local medical advice in order to ascertain whether any coral or sting remains in the wound. Such injuries take a long time to heal and can be liable to infection. The main diving resorts in Eilat (and across the Egyptian border in Sinai) have medical facilities equipped to deal with diving accidents.

If you get sick
Contact your embassy or consulate for a list of doctors and dentists who speak your language, or at least some English. Doctors and health facilities in major cities are also listed in the Directory sections of this book. Make sure you have adequate insurance.

Useful websites
www.btha.org British Travel Health Association.
www.cdc.gov US government site that gives excellent advice on travel health and details of disease outbreaks.
www.fco.gov.uk British Foreign and Commonwealth Office travel site has useful information on each country, people, climate and a list of UK embassies/consulates.
www.fitfortravel.scot.nhs.uk A-Z of vaccine/health advice for each country.
www.numberonehealth.co.uk Travel screening services, vaccine and travel health advice, email/SMS text vaccine reminders and screening returned travellers for tropical diseases.

Language
If the State of Israel represents the in-gathering of the Jewish people from the Diaspora, then the Hebrew language represents one of the main unifying factors. In fact, the very pronunciation of modern Israeli Hebrew (a compromise between Sephardi and Ashkenazi elements) symbolizes its unifying influence.

For several thousand years Hebrew was just used for Jewish liturgy. Indeed, there are some elements in Israeli society (most notably the ultra-orthodox community from Eastern Europe) who believe that it is blasphemous to use Hebrew outside of liturgy, and thus they continue to use native tongues (frequently Yiddish). The modern usage of Hebrew was revived largely through the efforts of Eliezer Ben Yehuda (1858-1922), with the modern Hebrew movement becoming appended to the early Zionist movement. Theodor Herzl is alleged to have wistfully remarked, "Can you imagine buying a train ticket in Hebrew?".

Hebrew is a West Semitic language related to Assyrian and Aramaic. As a general rule, an Israeli could read a Hebrew Bible with relative ease, whilst someone brought up on biblical Hebrew would have some difficulty reading an Israeli newspaper.

The second most widely spoken language is Arabic. It belongs to a branch of the southwestern branch of the Semitic language group, though there are a number of different dialects.

Road signs in Israel are almost always written in Hebrew and English, and in most areas Arabic too. English is widely spoken and understood, particularly by those involved in the tourist industry. The Diaspora experience is reflected in the number of other languages spoken in Israel, including Ethiopian, German, Yiddish, Polish, Romanian, Hungarian, Spanish, and notably Russian.

Money

Currency → *US$1 = 3.99 NIS, €1 = 4.94 NIS, £1 = 6.21 NIS (Aug 2012)*

The unit of currency in Israel is the New Israeli Shekel, written as NIS. It has in fact been 'new' for over 20 years. The Hebrew plural of shekel is shekelim, though the generally used expression is 'shekels' (or 'sheks'). The new shekel is divided into 100 agorot. There are notes of 200, 100, 50, 20NIS, plus coins of 10, 5, 2 and 1NIS. There are also coins of 50 and 10 agorot.

Note that by paying in foreign hard currencies (preferably US dollars) for hotel accommodation, car hire, airline tickets and expensive purchases, you avoid paying Value Added Tax (VAT). Though almost all foreign hard currencies are accepted, US Dollars remain the best option. It is always useful to have some hard currency cash with you, particularly when you are crossing borders. A mix of high and low denomination US dollars is probably the best bet.

Credit cards

Credit cards are accepted pretty much everywhere. Banks with ATMs are found in even the smallest towns. Debit/credit card withdrawals are the easiest and best way to access your travelling funds.

Changing money

Travellers' cheques and foreign currency can be cashed at banks and money-changers, though commission charges are excessive. Good places to change money are post offices (which all offer commission-free foreign exchange at good rates). You will need to bring your passport.

Licensed Arab money-changers near Jerusalem's Damascus Gate are also a good source of Jordanian dinars and Egyptian pounds for those travelling beyond Israel (something worth considering).

If you need to transfer money, most main post offices act as agents for Western Union. Commission charges are high, though. For further details, see www.westernunion.com.

Cost of travelling

Public transport in Israel is reasonably good value. As an example, the country's longest bus journey, the 6 hrs from Haifa to Eilat, is US$20. For further details, see page 10.

Your daily budget will be influenced by how much sightseeing and which activities you intend doing. Israeli national parks and general sights charge between nothing and US$10 for admission.

With careful budgeting it should be possible to eat, sleep and see something of the region on US$40-50 per day. You do meet some people surviving on US$20 a day, though they invariably seem to be miserable and tend to leave Israel having seen next to nothing.

Opening hours

Few first-time visitors to Israel are prepared for the impact of Shabbat, or the Jewish Sabbath. Beginning at sun-down on Fri and finishing at sun-down on Sat, it sees all Israeli offices, banks, post offices, and many shops, restaurants and places of entertainment close down completely. Almost everywhere, both the inter-city and urban transport systems grind to a complete halt, although taxis are available (for higher rates). If you don't want to get stranded somewhere, plan in advance for Shabbat. Note that in many work environments, the 'weekend' is now adding Fri to the Sat day of rest.

Safety

There are a number of security and safety considerations that should be borne in mind when visiting Israel. Though acts of terrorism have been rare in recent years, it remains a volatile country and violence can flare up as a result of any political provocation. Recently, incidents have occurred near the border between Egypt and Eilat. The security situation across the border in Sinai remains volatile, so keep yourself abreast of the political changes. Security forces are much in evidence throughout the country, with serves to reassure most visitors.

Being sensible and vigilant, though not over-paranoid, is the best way to approach the issue of safety in Israel.

Time

Israel is 2 hrs ahead of Greenwich Mean Time (GMT+2); 7 hrs ahead of American Eastern Standard Time; 8 hrs behind Australian Eastern Standard Time. Clocks go forward 1 hr for daylight-saving ('summer time') in Mar, and back again at Rosh Hashanah (usually Sep).

Tipping

In common with many other countries in the world, bar staff, waiters and waitresses in Israel receive fairly low wages, relying on tips to top up their salaries. If service is good then add 10%, if not leave nothing. It is not customary to tip taxi drivers. Tipping guides and tour bus drivers is a matter of personal choice. If someone cleans your room the right thing to do is leave a tip (5NIS per day is perfectly acceptable).

Tourist information

Visit www.visitisrael.gov.il
and www.touristisrael.com.

Visas and immigration

On arrival (by land or sea) you will be requested to fill in a landing card. If you request (but only if you specifically ask), the immigration official will stamp this card and not your passport. On arrival by air, you can request 'no stamp' also. The lack of a stamp will only cause you difficulties when crossing the border into Egypt or Jordan, when officials may delay you while they check everything is in order. This usually just involves a few phone calls being made. Note that you may have to provide evidence of a return ticket, though this is very rare.

Passports

All visitors require a passport that is valid for 6 months beyond the date of their entry into Israel. You should carry your passport with you (in a secure place) at all times. You may be required to show it when checking in to hotels. You will be asked for your passport at checkpoints if travelling around the West Bank.

Visas

Almost all nationalities are granted a free 3-month **tourist visa** on arrival, whether via land or air. The exceptions to this rule include most African countries, Arab/Muslim nations, India and many of the former Soviet republics. Be aware that at a land border you may be asked how long you intend to stay; then the exact figure you state could well be what you are issued with. Tourist visas do not permit you to work. They can be extended (see below). Visas expire on exit from Israel. For further details on arrival protocol see page 7.

If you are intending to work on a kibbutz or moshav, it is possible to apply for a 6-12 month volunteer visa once you are already inside Israel with the help of your kibbutz or moshav. Applicants should be aware that this visa is non-transferable, so if you move kibbutz you need a new visa.

A 12-month **student visa** is available to those who have been accepted by a university/education institute, though it is non-transferable and does not allow you to work. It is recommended to apply for the visa before arriving in Israel from an Israeli embassy abroad, though it is possible to obtain after arrival in the country if necessary. You require a letter of acceptance and proof of sufficient funds to cover tuition and living costs.

Jewish visitors considering returning to Israel permanently may be eligible for **temporary residence**. It is advisable that you contact one of the relevant agencies to guide you through this process: Association of **Americans and Canadians in Israel** (AACI), Jerusalem, T02-5661181, www.aaci.org.il; **British Olim Society**, 37 Pierre Koenig, Talpiyyot, Jerusalem, T02-5635244; 76 Ibn Gvirol, Tel Aviv, T03-6965244, www.ujia.org.il.

Contents

Footprint features

Background

Geography

The Negev, Hebrew for 'arid land', comprises over half of the State of Israel's land area, but is home to just 12% of the population. The Negev is shaped like an upside-down isosceles triangle, with the long sides being the Egyptian border to the west and the Jordanian border to the east, and the short side comprising a line drawn roughly between the Dead Sea to the east, and the Mediterranean Sea at Gaza to the west. The apex of the triangle is marked by the city of Eilat, on the Gulf of Aqaba.

History

Early history Despite the Negev's seemingly difficult and inhospitable nature, the region has been settled continuously since prehistoric times. During the Late Bronze Age-Iron Age I-II, the 19th and 20th dynasties of the **Egyptian** New Kingdom were involved in extensive copper mining and smelting activities in the southern Negev and Sinai regions, with the **Midianites** continuing this activity after the 12th century BCE.

Biblical references to Negev settlements abound, with excavations having revealed a rich assemblage of sites from the **Bronze Age** (c. 3300-1200 BCE) and the **Iron Age** (1200-586 BCE). The first five books of the Old Testament of the Bible, (*Genesis, Exodus, Leviticus, Numbers* and *Deuteronomy*) are filled with references to settlements in the Negev that have since been identified, such as Be'er Sheva (*Genesis 21:31-33; 26:23-33; 46:1-5*), Arad (*Numbers 21:1; 33:40*), Kadesh Barnea (*Genesis 14:7; Numbers 13:26; 20:14; Deuteronomy 1:46*), amongst others. This, after all, is the land of the route into Exodus, the return, and the wanderings of the Children of Israel.

By the beginning of the second millennium BCE, three main groups occupied the Negev: the **Canaanites** to the north, particularly around Arad; the **Amalekites** to the south, who were defeated by the United Monarchy's expansion into the Negev; and the **Edomites** to the east, who later moved north and northwest into the Shephelah, and subsequently became known as the Idumaeans.

The expansion of the **United Monarchy** (c. 1020-928 BCE) into the Negev Hills is reflected in a number of Iron Age IIA sites (1000-900 BCE), though the area was probably abandoned by the succeeding kings of Judah until the beginning of the Persian period (586 BCE). The reasons are not altogether clear, though the devastating invasion of Pharaoh Shishak in 924 BCE may have been a factor. Be'er Sheva (Beersheba), for example, is repeatedly mentioned in the Bible as defining the southern limits of Israel, the United Monarchy, or Judah (*Joshua 15:28; I Samuel 3:20; II Samuel 3:10, 17:11, 24:15; I Chronicles 21:2*). Other areas of the Negev remained occupied: Arad, for example, has remains of a series of Israelite citadels dating from the ninth to the sixth centuries BCE.

The Nabateans Perhaps one of the key defining moments in the history of the Negev was the arrival of the Nabateans, some time in the fourth or third century BCE. Their origins are unclear, though their impact is undisputed. As controllers of the trade route, the Spice Road, between their Edom capital at Petra and the Mediterranean Sea at Gaza, the Nabateans constructed a string of road stations across the Negev, spectacular remains of which can still be seen today. Their mastery of advanced irrigation techniques, in particular their control of surface water run-off, led to the establishment of urban centres of considerable size, such as Oboda (Avdat), Mamphis (Mamshit), Sobata (Shivta), and to a lesser extent, Elusa (Haluza) and Nessana (Nizzana).

Roman and Byzantine periods The independent Nabatean empire probably reached its peak in the first century CE, though the towns and routes that they established seem to have been little affected by the annexation of their kingdom into the Roman *Provincia Arabia* in 106 CE. In fact, the majority of the population of these towns were ethnically Nabatean and, as such, the Early Roman period (37 BCE-132 CE) may accurately be referred to here as the Middle Nabatean period.

A major administrative reorganization of the Eastern Roman Empire under **Diocletian** (284-305 CE) incorporated many of the Nabatean towns within the empire's southern defence system. New trade routes also led to the rise or demise of certain Nabatean towns.

The major development in the Negev region during the fourth century CE was the conversion of much of the population to Christianity. Thus ushered in the **Byzantine period** (324-638 CE), during which many of the former Nabatean towns flourished, with the monumental churches that can be seen today bearing testimony to this prosperity. The decline of Byzantine power allowed the Arabs to conquer the Negev in 636 CE, and for the next 1000 years or so, the region was inhabited solely by the **Bedouin**.

Modern history The Negev region remained a relative backwater of the Ottoman Empire right up until the **First World War**, when its strategic value was recognized. The British Army's Palestine campaign featured largely in the northern and western areas of the Negev, with Be'er Sheva being the first town in Palestine to fall into British hands (1917). In addition to General Allenby's campaign, this was also the stomping ground of TE Lawrence ('of Arabia'). Before his wartime efforts at disrupting Turkish communications and supply lines, Lawrence had spent much of 1914 surveying the archaeological sites of the area for the Palestine Exploration Fund. After the war, the Negev fell within the mandated area of the British, though there were few attempts to develop it. Population levels still remained extremely low, comprising mainly Bedouin tribesmen. In fact, the **Peel Commission Partition Plan** of 1937 granted the Negev region to the Arabs since they represented the only people living there.

Partially in response to this situation, and partially out of a desire to settle the region that Moses wandered through with the Children of Israel, Jewish pioneers began to establish isolated communities within the Negev. This programme was to prove significant in its foresight in later years. By the time the **United Nations Partition Recommendation** was published in 1947, the presence of these isolated Jewish communities was enough for the UN to allocate the entire Negev region (bar a narrow strip to the south of Gaza) to the Jewish State. With the Arab rejection of the plan, and the subsequent war, these Jewish settlements played an invaluable, and often heroic, role in holding up the Egyptian army's advance. In one of the final acts of the war, the Golani Brigade managed to establish control of a stretch of the Gulf of Aqaba (subsequently Eilat), that allowed Israel an outlet to the Red Sea.

There remains much controversy over Israel's claims that it has 'turned the desert green', but there can be little doubt that Israel leads the world in developing semi-arid and arid irrigation techniques. Thus, large areas of the Negev have been brought under cultivation. The results of establishing 'development towns' in the Negev are more contentious; for every 'success' (see Arad), the example of at least one 'failure' (see Dimona) is held up. **Tourism** is now providing a major source of income in the Negev region.

Northern Negev

The Northern Negev has a number of points of interest to the visitor, particularly those who have their own transport. The commercial capital of the Negev, Be'er Sheva, is an easy-going place, with several interesting attractions in the immediate vicinity. The bulk of the sights, however, lie to the east and southeast of Be'er Sheva, notably the archaeological sites at Tel Arad and Mamshit. For those with their own vehicles, the Makhtesh HaGadol and Makhtesh HaKatan (craters) provide a wonderfully scenic backdrop to a number of hikes.

Be'er Sheva (Beersheba) → *For listings, see pages 31-33.*

The ancient biblical city of the patriarchs, Be'er Sheva is redefining itself as the modern administrative and commercial capital of the Negev. Attractions in the town itself are limited and, though there are good transport connections, its potential as a base from which to explore the surrounding area is constrained by the limited choice of hotels. However, the Old City downtown area has a relaxed, laid-back atmosphere, with restoration of the Ottoman architecture ongoing and some nice restaurants opening up. Be'er Sheva's headlong rush for expansion can be seen in the numerous tower blocks shooting up, and modern architecture that embraces plate glass, angles and colourful panels. The university is highly regarded these days and hence the student population is swelling, which means Be'er Sheva is increasingly known as a place for a good night out.

Arriving in Be'er Sheva (Beersheba)

Getting there and away Most visitors arrive at the large Central Bus Station located just off Derekh Eilat. Be'er Sheva has good bus connections, with major destinations such as Eilat, Ein Gedi, Jerusalem and Tel Aviv being served by express, regular and local (Metropoline) buses. There is a fast train service between Be'er Sheva and Tel Aviv (and beyond), and it's a relaxing journey though more expensive than the bus. The train station is located immediately next to the bus station, with another stop near the university north of the centre.

Getting around The town centre is fairly small, so you can easily get around on foot. The local Metropoline routes around town (4NIS) leave next to the Central Bus Station, running regularly from 0520-2300. For details of Metropoline buses, T*5900.

Tourist information The **Visitors' Centre** ① *Abraham's Well, 1 Hebron Rd, T08-6234613, bavraham@br7.orgi.il, Sun-Thu 0800-1600, Friday 0830-1230*, has a good map of the city (5NIS), leaflets about sights in the area and a gift shop. Worth a visit.

Background

Ancient history and biblical references There are numerous biblical references to the early settlement of Be'er Sheva (Beersheba), with the etymology of the name being discussed in *Genesis*. The meaning of the name may refer to either the 'Well of Seven' (see 'Abraham's Well', page 28) from the Hebrew *shiv'a*, or 'Well of (the) Oath' from the Hebrew *shevu'a*, with the origin of Beersheba attributed to both Abraham (*Genesis 21:29-33*) and Isaac (*Genesis 26:15-33*). Jacob received the vision here that told him to take his family into Egypt (*Genesis 46:1-2*); the city was a place of importance under Samuel, with his sons Joel and Abiah judging here (*I Samuel 8:1-2*); and Elijah fled here from Jezreel on his journey to Mount Horeb (*I Kings 19:3*).

Many of the biblical references mention Beersheba as the limits of the kingdom of Judah (*Joshua 15:28*), the lands of Israel (*I Samuel 3:20*) and the United Monarchy (*II Samuel 3:10, 17:11, 24:15; I Chronicles 21:2*), with the most common incantations being 'from Dan to Beersheba' and 'from Beersheba to Dan'.

Excavations at a site known as **Tel Be'er Sheva**, 5 km northeast of the modern city (see page 35), have revealed levels of occupation dating back to the Iron Age. However, identification of the tel with biblical Beersheba has been problematic due to the lack of remains dating to the Late Bronze and Late Iron Age periods that would coincide with the Beersheba of the patriarchs.

Much of Be'er Sheva's history during the **Persian period** and the **Roman-Byzantine period** is told at the site of Tel Be'er Shev.

Ottoman Empire and British Mandate The Crusaders never made it as far south as here, mistaking the site of Bet Jibrin (Bet Guvrin) for biblical Beersheba. It was the Turks who revived Be'er Sheva's fortunes at the turn of the 20th century, establishing a new town to act as an administrative centre for the Bedouin tribes of the Negev, thus strengthening the declining Ottoman Empire. Jewish settlement also began during this period. The British forces of General Allenby captured the town in 1917 as part of the World War One Palestine campaign. It subsequently expanded rapidly, with the population rising to around 7000.

The British government's White Paper of 1943 forbade the Jewish purchase of land in the Negev, though the reality of isolated Jewish settlements in the Negev convinced the architects of the 1947 United Nations Partition Plan to include most of the Negev within the proposed Jewish state. Be'er Sheva, however, was just within the boundaries of the proposed Arab state. When war broke out following the declaration of the State of Israel, Be'er Sheva was occupied by the Egyptians, who established their command centre here. The city was subsequently captured by the Negev Brigade of the Israeli army in October 1948.

Modern city The initiative for transforming the city into the administrative and commercial capital of the Negev was taken by the city's first mayor, David Tuvyahu. The population of Be'er Sheva is now around 185,000, helped in no small part by the massive influx of immigrants that followed the city's designation as an 'immigration absorption city'. In addition to Moroccan and Ethiopian Jews, the city is home to a sizeable and highly visible Eastern European community. Apparently around 160 languages are spoken in the schools and markets of the city.

Places in Be'er Sheva (Beersheba)

Walking tour of the Old City Many of Be'er Sheva's places of interest are located in the attractive Old City area, the grid pattern of streets built by the Turks as their regional headquarters around the turn of the 20th century. A walking tour of the Old City, taking in mainly Ottoman and British Mandate period buildings, starts at the Visitors' Centre and takes around one hour. The Be'er Sheva map, available from the Visitors' Centre (5NIS), gives additional information to that given here. You may feel that some of the 'attractions' on the walking tour are not worth the effort.

Abraham's Well (1) ① *Entrance 5NIS. See Visitors' Centre, above.* "And Abimelech said unto Abraham, What mean these seven ewe lambs which thou hast set by themselves? And he said, For these seven ewe lambs shalt thou take of my hand, that they may be a witness unto me, that I have digged this well. Wherefore he called that place Beersheba; because there they sware both of them… And Abraham planted a grove in Beersheba, and called there on the name of the Lord, the everlasting God." (*Genesis 21:29-33*). And, lo,

Be'er Sheva Centre & Old City

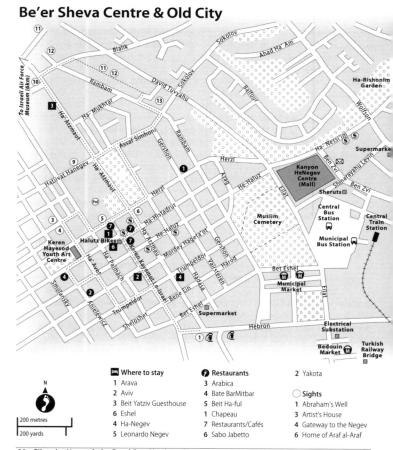

🛏 Where to stay	☕ Restaurants	2 Yakota
1 Arava	3 Arabica	
2 Aviv	4 Bate BarMitbar	◯ Sights
3 Beit Yatziv Guesthouse	5 Beit Ha-ful	1 Abraham's Well
6 Eshel	1 Chapeau	3 Artist's House
4 Ha-Negev	7 Restaurants/Cafés	4 Gateway to the Negev
5 Leonardo Negev	6 Sabo Jabetto	6 Home of Araf al-Araf

so it came to pass that a certain well, thought to be 12th century CE, with water-drawing constructions dating to the Ottoman period, is named after the patriarch. The ticket price also includes a short movie sketching the history of Be'er Sheva to the modern day, and a guided explanation of the site (available Sun-Thu until 1400). Look out for the 500-year-old 'eshel' (tamarisk) tree just outside the walls.

Negev Artists House (3) ① *55 HaAvot, T08-6273828, Mon-Thu 1000-1330 and 1600-1930, Fri 1000-1330, Sat 1100-1400.* This Mandate period building now displays work by Negev artists, both Bedouin and Jewish, new immigrants and old, in a variety of mediums. Occasionally there are musical, poetry or literary evenings. Artworks are for sale, and there is an interesting choice of ceramics, painting, jewellery, weaving, etching, etc available.

The former Turkish government building, **Bet Hasseraya (5)**, is adorned with much barbed wire and is used by the Israeli military (no photography); adjacent is the memorial at **Allenby Garden (7)**.

Ottoman period buildings On the pedestrianized Keren Kayemet Le-Israel, you pass a number of restored buildings from the Ottoman period; the most notable being the building at No 94 that now serves as the HaNegev Pharmacy. At the junction of Herzl and Ha'Atzma'ut is the former home of the Arab historian **Araf al-Araf (6)** (1892-1973), who also served as a district ruler under the Ottomans, which has been splendidly restored. A more inglorious fate has befallen the former home of Sheikh Brich Abu-Medin, Bedouin sheikh, British-appointed Mayor of Be'er Sheva, and Bedouin representative to the British government. His former house on the junction of Ha'Atzma'ut and Ha-Histadrut is now a discount clothes shop.

Negev Art Museum (8) ① *Remez Gardens, 60 Ha'Atzma'ut, T08-6206570, Sun, Mon, Wed and Thu 0800-1530, Tue 0800-1400 and 1600-1800, Fri 1000-1400. Adult 14NIS, student/child 10NIS.* Housed in the former Turkish **Governor's Residence**, a mansion built in 1906 that later served as Be'er Sheva's first City Hall, the Art Museum has recently been cleverly restored and modified. The result is an attractive melding of modern glass intimate galleries into the original Turkish design. The museum features temporary

To Ben Gurion
University & Tel Aviv

Montefiori

Nessim

issta

Henrietta Szold

Ha-Tivot

Mall

Keren Ha-Yesod

□ Supermarket

To big Shopping Centre (2km),
Tel Be'er Sheva (6km), Arad
47km & Dead Sea

Hebron

6 Home of Araf al-Araf	**10** World War 1 Cemetery
8 Negev Art Museum	**9** Bedouin School
13 Water Tower	**7** Allenby Garden
12 Turkish Railway Station	**5** Bet Hasseraya
11 Turkish Station Master's House	-------- Route of walking tour of old city

Bedouin of the Negev

The Negev's Bedouin community numbers approximately 180,000, mainly concentrated in seven townships established by the Israeli government. These towns are designed to concentrate the Bedouin population and much of their traditional lands have been confiscated to make way for military zones, Jewish communities, and national parks. Nomadic Bedouin are a thing of the past, and the younger generation know little of the traditional ways. Many people today call themselves 'Palestinian Bedouin'.

The largest town is Rehad, 50 km north of Be'er Sheva, home to some 50,000 people. A further 65,000 Bedouin have chosen to remain in the 'unrecognized' villages that dot the roads around Be'er Sheva and Arad. The villages are deemed illegal since, although the Bedouin own their land, large tracts were not registered and are defined as 'state land' by the authorities. House demolitions are a real threat and the Israeli government sometimes destroys an entire village in one day. Generally constructed of metal sheeting, these settlements are not provided with municipal services such as electricity lines, garbage collection

or running water, though some have electricity generators and a communal water supply. Their children attend school in the 'official' townships. Do visit a village if driving past, introduce yourself to whoever you meet and perhaps you'll experience the traditional Bedouin hospitality.

The Bedouin have Israeli citizenship but are exempt from army service (although 5-10% of draft age youth do volunteer for the army). Currently they have one member in the Knesset, and clan members are permitted to visit family in Sinai. However, the settlement process has not come with access to their traditional lands or permission to make a living through agriculture. They likewise have had little access to grazing land since large tracts of the Negev were declared a National Park in 1979. It is unsurprising that employment is rife and crime levels are extremely high (you are advised not to leave a car unattended in rural areas of the Negev). Most Bedouin still work the land and tend flocks of goat and sheep, however many work as construction labourers, and a few benefit from visiting tourists.

Compiled with the assistance of Fred Schlomka, www.greenolivetours.com.

art exhibitions by Israeli and international artists, in various mediums, which change every three months. Just next door is a renovated **Ottoman mosque** (6), also built in 1906, with the insignia of Sultan Abdul Hamid II above the door. It is currently a controversial subject, as the Muslim community wish to use it again as a mosque while the municipality intended it for use as the archaeological wing of the museum. It used to house archaeological finds from the Be'er Sheva region, Tel Sheva in particular, which are now in the Israel Museum in Jerusalem.

Former Bedouin School (9) This building was erected by the Turks in 1913 for use as a boarding school for Bedouin boys, and during World War One was used as a military hospital. The building is undergoing a major refurbishment and will be part of a Youth Science Park.

World War One cemetery (10) During the autumn of 1917, the Allied forces broke through the Turkish lines and captured Be'er Sheva. The battle was not without cost, and today 1239 Allied soldiers are buried here, the biggest World War One cemetery in Israel. Many of the graves belong to members of Commonwealth regiments, with Australians and New

Zealanders buried next to Welsh and English soldiers. A lot of graves are simply marked 'A Soldier of the Great War'. As with all cemeteries administered by the Commonwealth War Graves Commission, it is superbly maintained.

Turkish railway remains The northernmost section of the walking tour features a series of buildings connected with the old Turkish railway. This is the line that features so prominently in the writing and exploits of Lawrence of Arabia. The track was dismantled by General Allenby in 1917, but it is possible here to see the former **Turkish Station Master's House (11)**, and **Turkish Railway Station (12)**, now both in a poor state of repair and fenced off. The original station platform remains. Further south still, but now hidden amongst a residential area, is the **water-tower (13)** used to fill the trains' boilers.

Bedouin Market
An abundant underground water supply and a central location on the trade routes were the two main reasons that Be'er Sheva grew into an important town in antiquity. Active commerce continues unabated and there has been a weekly Bedouin market in Be'er Sheva since 1905, though the exact location has changed on several occasions. The market now takes place each **Thursday** (0700-sunset) at the grounds on the north bank of the Nahal Be'er Sheva, just off the Eilat Road. Although there are Bedouin wares on sale (jewellery, ceramics, rugs, clothes, fabrics and copperware), to many this market is no more exotic than the average car-boot sale. Long gone are the days when you could buy hashish, slaves, pure silk or women at the market, but you can get pretty much anything else. To the south of the market grounds you can see the **Turkish Bridge**. Closer to the bus station (under the arched covers) is the daily municipal market, which is also a good place to stock up on cheap goods.

Be'er Sheva listings

For hotel and restaurant price codes and other relevant information, see pages 12-16.

Where to stay
$$$ Leonardo Negev, 4 Henrietta Szold, T08-6405444, www.fattal.co.il. Tower-block hotel aimed at business-people. Not much to choose between 'regular' and 'business' rooms save for the decor (more modern and attractive). All have fridge, desk, minibar and nice bathrooms. Mini-suite with sitting room and 2 Presidential suites (**$$$$**) with kitchenette and jacuzzi. Lobby café-bar gives new meaning to the word 'spacious'. Fully equipped gym, sauna and jacuzzi, large outdoor pool. Good facilities, without the real feel of luxury.
$$ Arava, 37 Ha-Histadrut, T08-6278792. Not much English spoken but friendly, ancient Eastern Europeans seem to be main

clientele (and decor to match), modest rooms a bit shabby but very clean, attached bath (at lower end of **$$** price category).
$$ Aviv, 48 Mordey HaGeta'ot, T08-6278059. Simple but spotlessly clean, new sheets and flowery theme, TV, a/c, private bath, front rooms with (scruffy) balconies. No breakfast but free tea/coffee in the sunny reception, nice family, some English spoken. Recommended for those on a budget. Single/twin/double 150/200/250NIS.
$$ Beit Yatziv Guesthouse, 79 Ha'Atzma'ut, T08-6277444, www.beityatziv.co.il. Very well maintained a/c 3- or 4-bed rooms with TV and fridge, but quite expensive and not permitted to take a 'dorm bed', you have to come as 3 or 4 people together (120-130NIS per person). More luxy rooms range from 250/350NIS (single/double) to 400NIS (single and double). Set in a campus of the open university with pleasant grounds,

a dining room (lunch/dinner 50NIS) and huge swimming pool plus paddling pools (summer only, outside guests 25-35NIS). No curfew, 24-hr reception. The staff are very off-hand but it's the nicest choice in town. On entering the campus, turn left to find the guesthouse.

$$ HaNegev, 26 Ha'Atzma'ut, T08-6277026. Double rooms 200-250NIS, those in annex are rather musty though they have TV; better rooms in new block are quite big with a/c, attached bath, towels but need to request top-sheet. None are impressive but it is more 'normal' than the other cheapies and clean enough.

$ Eshel, 56 Ha-Histadrut, T08-6272917. This old-fashioned time-warp place is a real oddity, but rooms are clean and cheap (singles 120NIS, doubles 150NIS) with towels, sheets, fresh paint. Communication via pen and paper. There's a shower in the room (literally), toilet outside.

Restaurants

There's a fair mix of interesting restaurants in Be'er Sheva. **The Kanyon HaNegev Centre** (Sun-Thu 0900-2200, Fri 0900-1500) has a handy Aroma (with wireless connection) serving the usual light meals. Inside/outside the central bus station are numerous bakeries, falafel, shwarma places. The main square at the north end of the pedestrianized **Keren Kayemet Le-Israel** is a good place to sit with your falafel or shwarma. If you're doing it yourself, there are several supermarkets in both the old and new city, with fresh fruit and vegetables in abundance at the Municipal market. **Beer-Teva**, in the empty mall next to the Leonardo hotel, T1-800-225577, has organic health foods (Sun-Thu 0900-2000, Fri 0900-1400).

$$$-$$ Chapeau, 81 Herzl, T08-6551811. Sun-Thu 1000-0100, Fri 1000-1400, Sat from 2000. Dairy restaurant, serves, excellent pastas, light meals and fish dishes. The entirely white environment sets off a goblet of red wine perfectly, and there's a covered terrace at the front with a slight trattoria vibe. No English menu or sign.

$$$-$$ Yakota, 18 Mordey Hagetaot, T08-6232689. Daily 1200-0030. Moroccan restaurant with a gorgeously styled interior, intimate layout, lovely lamps and cushions, very romantic. Some of the dishes are positively scary, however, involving spleen, tonsils, feet and testicles. Perhaps opt for the slow-cooked casseroles, generous salad selections (35NIS, 2 persons, for 12 samples), fish (88-96NIS) or vegetarian meals (40-60NIS). Alcohol served.

$$ Arabica, T08-6277801. Daily 1200-2400. A real everything menu, from sushi to steak via pasta and burgers. The salad bar is a good deal. A fairly anonymous setting, cavernous with echoes of a theme-pub, but it's not overpriced, is open on Shabbat and it's lively.

$$ Mate BaMitbar, 22 Ha-Histadrut, T08-6233370. Sun-Thu 0900-2330, Fri 0900-1400, Sat 2000-2330. Within the Bet Hanegbi. This former home of the first military ruler of Be'er Sheva after the 1948 war has been turned into a charming restaurant with garden-terrace space, simple decor, dairy kosher food and light meals. Very relaxing, especially if you make use of the spa in the same building.

$$-$ Beit Ha-Ful, 15 Ha-Histadrut, T08-6234253. Excellent value, with Be'er Sheva's best fuul, hummus, falafel and shwarma. Dishes come with overwhelming amounts of pickles, salads and dips. Recommended.

$$-$ Saba Jabeto, 8 Rasko Passage, T08-6272829. Sun-Thu 0930-2400, Fri 1000-1600, Sat 2030-2400. Handily opposite the bus station, 'Grandpa Jabeto's' coffee bar is so much more than coffee. Every combination of sandwich filling you can imagine, mostly in ciabatta bread, plus Indian options, Tunisian options, stir-fry options, healthy options, all 28-35NIS. Also quiches, omelettes, great slushies, alcohol, plus a nice welcoming environment to relax. Ask staff what the special deals are.

Bars and clubs

When it comes to nighttime entertainment, Be'er Sheva is rather deceptive. What appears to be a sleepy, quiet town has quite a number of lively bars and cafés. The whole area around **Keren Kayemet Le-Israel** has a number of pleasant evening-time watering holes, whilst those seeking a younger vibe should head north to the university area and the bars on **Ringelblum** and **Yosef Ben Mattithiau** (ask students to direct you to Pablo pub, Einstein or Inca bar). The BIG shopping mall, just east of the town centre along the Hebron road, has numerous watering holes, and **Draft Dance-bar** is recommended.

What to do
Gym

Non-guests can use the gym, sauna and jacuzzis at the **Leonardo** hotel (Sun-Thu 0700-2200, Fri 0700-1800, Sat 0700-1800, 30NIS).

Swimming

Non-guests can pay to use the pool at **Beit Yatziv Guesthouse**, summer only (25-35NIS).

Tour operators

Egged Tours, Central Bus Station, T6232532; issta, 8 Henrietta Szold, T08-6650288, Sun-Thu 0900-1900, Fri 0900-1300.

Transport
Bus

The town centre is fairly small, so you can easily get around on foot. Local buses (4NIS) leave from the **Municipal bus station**, with most running regularly from 0520-2300. They also make stops in the Old City, along Ha'Atzma'ut.

Long-distance buses The **Central Bus Station** is located off Derekh Eilat, right in the middle of town. The bus information office is particularly unhelpful but the electronic display board is useful. Main destinations such as **Eilat**, **Jerusalem** and **Tel Aviv** are served by express, regular and local buses. Actual departure times may change during

the lifetime of this book, but they still serve as a guide to the frequency of the services. **Arad**: Bus 388 direct, 2-3 per hr, Sun-Thu 0600-2315, Fri 0600-1645, Sat from 1945, 45 mins; **Ashqelon**: Bus 363/364, Sun-Thu 0615-2130, Fri 0615-1515, Sat 2000-2245; **Dimona**: Bus 48/56/397, 2 per hr, Sun-Thu 0600-2300, Fri 0600-1630, Sat 1745-2330; **Eilat**: Bus 392/393/394/397, Sun-Thu 0730-1835, Fri last at 1735, Sat 1745-2135, 3-4 hrs; **Ein Gedi** Bus 384 Sun-Thu 0930, 1215, 1500, Fri 0945, 1250, Sat 0940, 1215, 1500; **Jerusalem**: Bus 470 direct, Sun-Thu 1 per hr 0605-1950, Fri 0615-1300, Sat 2000-2215, 2 hrs; Jerusalem via **Kiryat Arba** (Hebron): Bus 440, Sun-Thu 0555, 1035, Fri 0930; Jerusalem via Kiryat Gat: Bus 446, 2 per hr, Sun-Thu 0600-2130, Fri 0720-1600, Sat 2010-2245; **Lahav**: Bus 42/47, Sun-Thu 1150, 1900; **Mizpe Ramon**: Egged bus 392 (to Eilat), Sun-Thu 0815, 0915, 1200, 1545, Fri 0800, 1 hr, and Metropoline bus 60 via Sde Boker/Avdat1-2 per hr, Sun-Thu 0615-2300, Fri 0615-1630, Sat 1900, 2030, 2210, 2300; **Tel Aviv**: Bus 369/370/371, every 15 mins, Sun-Thu 0510-2300, Fri 0510-1630, Sat from 1700.

Sheruts run to **Eilat**, **Jerusalem** and **Tel Aviv** from outside the Central Bus Station (same fare as bus), but they only depart when full.

Car hire

Avis, 2 Amal, Machteshim Industrial Zone, T0-6271777, www.avis.co.il; **Budget**, 1 Shazar Blvd, 03-9350017, www.budget.co.il; **Eldan**, 4 Leonard Cohen, T08-6430344, www.eldan.co.il.

Train

A comfortable and convenient option, the train station is next to the bus station especially the new superfast train from Tel Aviv. To **Tel Aviv** Sun-Thu at least 1 per hr 0525-2125, Fri last at 1220, Sat 2050, 1 hr; some services continue all the way to **Nahariyya**. To Dimona, Sun-Thu 0727, 1127, 1727, 1927, Fri 0820, 0920, 1120, 30 mins.

Around Be'er Sheva

Negev-Palmach Brigade Memorial (Andarta Memorial)

ⓘ T08-6463600.

Designed by the innovative Israeli artist Dani Karavan (also responsible for the Holocaust Memorial at Rehovot's Weizmann Institute of Science), this unusual work serves as a memorial to the Negev Brigade of the Palmach that distinguished itself in the 1948 War of Independence. Various parts of the sculpture symbolize different aspects of the campaign, with Hebrew inscriptions giving blow-by-blow accounts of the battles. The memorial is on the Be'er Sheva plateau, overlooking the Be'er Sheva Valley, though it can be difficult to reach by public transport. Off Be'er Sheva-Omer Road, several kilometres out of town to the northeast.

Be'er Sheva to Mizpe Ramon

Tel Be'er Sheva

ⓘ *T08-6467286, www.parks.org.il. Daily 0800-1700, winter 0800-1600, closes 1 hr earlier on Fri. Adults 14NIS, students/child 7NIS. Located on the Be'er Sheva to Omer-Hebron road (Route 60) 5 km northeast of the modern city. There is no public transport to the site.*

The most impressive remains on view at Tel Be'er Sheva today are from the Iron Age city, of which some two-thirds have been excavated. Declared a UNESCO World Heritage Site, mud bricks have been used to reconstruct many of the buildings and it is possible to get a clear picture of the heavily fortified Israelite city – especially from the top of the high observation tower. Good information is provided in the leaflet for the site.

Tour of the site Much of what you see today is from stratum III, and its continuation, stratum II, the latter being destroyed in a violent conflagration probably dating to the Assyrian king Sennacherib's campaign in 701 BCE. The main (and only) city gate probably dates to the 10th century BCE. Two guard rooms stand on either side, and it was protected by an outer gate. An irrigation channel runs through the city gate to a 70-m-deep well outside. This well is thought to date to the 12th century BCE, though it is curious why it was not enclosed within the latter city walls. There is even a view among some scholars that this may be the Well of Abraham that is mentioned in *Genesis 21:27-32*.

The city gate emerges on to the city square, to the west of which is the Governor's Residence. Note how the entrance is built using ashlars, rectangular hewn stones laid in horizontal courses, whereas the rest of the site is built from field stones. The building contains two dwelling units, a kitchen and storerooms. The cellar below may have previously formed part of a temple site.

To the right (east) of the city gate is the largest building: three pillared structures that probably formed part of the city storehouse. Broken pottery vessels attest to their usage, with commentators suggesting that these storage facilities were part of a taxation system established by Solomon. Stones from a horned altar were found incorporated into one of the storeroom walls. The original reconstructed horned altar now stands in the Israel Museum in Jerusalem but you can see a replica here, near the ticket booth. The interesting aspect of this altar is the fact that the stones were cut (ie it was 'horned'). Biblical law is quite strict in saying that the altar should be made from uncut stone: "And there thou shalt build an altar unto the Lord thy God, an altar of stones: thou shalt not lift any iron tool upon them" (*Deuteronomy 27:5*); and again, "an altar of whole stones, over which no man hath lift up any iron" (*Joshua 8:31*). The altar was probably broken up during the religious reforms of Hezekiah, King of Judah (727-698 BCE).

Also to be seen on the tel are a number of later ruins, the most noticeable of which is the rhomboid-shaped Roman fortress around the base of the observation tower. A tour of Tel Be'er Sheva finishes with a walk through the remarkably well-preserved water system, where the reservoir walls are layered with thick plaster and the chambers are quite magnificent.

Israeli Air Force Museum, Hazerim

ⓘ *T08-6906855. Sun-Thu 0800-1700, Fri 0800-1300. Adult 30NIS, student 23NIS, child 20NIS. The museum is located 7 km west of Be'er Sheva on Route 2357. Bus 31 goes hourly to Hazerim from the bus station (15 mins, 8.5NIS). Get off when you see the planes.*

This open-air museum features almost 100 assorted planes parked on a huge airfield. Guided tours, with a young soldier, last one to 1½ hours and make the experience infinitely more rewarding (phone to schedule a time), though you are welcome to visit alone and there are lots of information boards in English. There is a short film telling the story and glory of the Israeli Air Force (IAF), screened inside the belly of a Boeing 707 that played a minor role in the 1977 rescue at Entebbe, Uganda.

Lakia village

The Bedouin village of Lakia, on Route 31 about 6 km north of Be'er Sheva, is well worth a visit for anyone interested in the Bedouin way of life – and anyone interested in shopping for quality Bedouin handiwork. The **Desert Embroidery Project and Visitor Center** ① *T08-6513208, phone to arrange a visit, www.desert-embroidery.org*, provides employment and a source of income to local women, whilst preserving traditional embroidery designs and ensuring age-old skills are not lost. Tours can be arranged which include time in the Bedouin tent hearing about the lives and situation of the women and their families. There's a wide range of colourful bags, cushions, tablecloths, etc decorated with colourful designs for sale in a wide range of bright weaves and desert colours, using both contemporary and traditional designs. These workshops provide a rare opportunity to buy these desirable products which, ironically, are hard to track down in the Negev.

Joe Alon Centre: Museum of Bedouin Culture

① *Kibbutz Lahav, T08-9918597, www.joealon.org.il. Sat-Thu 0900-1700, Fri 0900-1400. Adult 20NIS. To reach the museum, head north from Be'er Sheva for 21 km on Route 40. Turn right at Dvira Jct on to Route 3255 and follow signs to the museum (8 km). By public transport, bus 42 runs from Be'er Sheva to Kibbutz Lahav nearby at 1150 (Sun-Thu only), but goes straight back again, so you would need to hitch back.*

Within the Joe Alon Regional and Folklore Centre is the 'Museum of Bedouin Culture', an attempt to explain aspects of the traditional Bedouin way of life (and their present day situation). Activities such as cooking, bread-baking, the coffee ceremony and carpet weaving are demonstrated, whilst displays present artefacts such as jewellery, clothing, agricultural implements and household utensils. Many of the items have been donated by the various Bedouin tribes of the Negev and the Sinai, with some of the things on display having now gone out of general usage. There is also a short movie about Bedouin life and donkey rides for children.

East and southeast of Be'er Sheva

From Be'er Sheva, it is possible to take one of two routes towards the Dead Sea Region. The east route takes in the Canaanite/Israelite city at Tel Arad and its modern neighbour Arad, before dropping below sea level down to the Dead Sea at Neve Zohar.

The southeast route to the Dead Sea, with a number of diversions, passes the modern town of Dimona, the ancient Nabatean city of Mamshit, and the two smaller of the Negev's three main craters, Makhtesh HaGadol and Makhtesh HaKatan. If travelling with your own transport, with an early start it is possible to take in the best of both routes in one grand loop that can return you to Be'er Sheva the same day. If relying on public transport, it would take several days to cover the key sites (with some remoter areas not accessible at all).

The Cave in the Mountain

① *Drejat village, contact Jaber Abu Hamad, T054-7969576, gabera66@gmail.com, www. drejat.lanegev.co.il. Drejat is 3.5 km north of Route 31 (the turn-off is about 5 km after Tel Arad Jct, when coming from Arad).*

On the edge of the Arad valley, at the base of the Yattir mountains, lies the Bedouin village of Drejat, established by 'falakhim' (Arab peasants) in the 19th century. The first villagers inhabited cave dwellings, and it is this heritage and way of life that Jaber Abu Hamad shares with visitors today. Discussions don't just dwell on the past, but cover the present day process of 'modernization' that Bedouin communities are undergoing: he transition from the old ways, from caves and a nomadic tent existence, to makeshift metal huts or (in some cases) plush housing. The famed Bedouin hospitality is mixed with storytelling, a visit to the remains of a Roman road, scenic observation points and of course sweet tea, bitter coffee and tabun bread (traditional 'farmers' meals can be ordered). Individual visitors are probably best to call ahead to see if they can join a bigger group. The Israel National Trail also passes the village.

Tel Arad

ⓘ *Daily 0800-1700, closes 1 hr earlier on Fri. Adult 14NIS, student/child 7NIS.*

At one time the site of the most important city in the Negev, Tel Arad has substantial remains from both the Canaanite and the later Israelite settlements. The site has been considerably restored, particularly the Israelite (and later) citadel at the top of the hill, which has been largely rebuilt using original material. The lower Canaanite city is the largest, most complete Early Bronze Age city yet excavated in Israel. The scenic views from the Israelite tower, with Bedouin villages dotting the South Hebron Hills and swathes of bright green cultivation to the east, is impressive. It is appealingly desolate and you are likely to be alone at the site, save for the numerous lizards. There is a nice picnic area and a campsite is being created.

Arriving in Tel Arad

Getting there and away Buses between Be'er Sheva and Arad (along Route 31) will drop you at Tel Arad Junction, the turning for the site, from where it is a 2.5-km walk (or hitch) to the site. Buses from Tel Aviv also pass the junction.

Background

The Canaanite city probably reached its peak towards the beginning of the Early Bronze Age II (3000-2700 BCE). The economy of the city was based primarily on agriculture, including production and processing of barley, wheat, peas, lentils, flax and olives, plus the rearing of livestock. Another important sector of the economy involved extensive trade with southern Sinai, Egypt and other Canaanite cities. Many of the jars, cooking pots and other artefacts found at Tel Arad are now in the Israel Museum in Jerusalem. Evidence from Stratum III (c. 2950-2800 BCE) suggests that much of the town was destroyed in some major conflagration, almost certainly the result of an enemy attack. The town appears to have been rebuilt almost immediately, though occupation was not to last long, with the city being abandoned by 2650 BCE. The reasons for this are not entirely clear, though climatic change, Egyptian encroachment or political unrest throughout Canaan have all been suggested. The fact that the Canaanite city site itself was never reoccupied explains why the remains are so extensive and well preserved.

After a gap of around 1600 years, parts of the site were reoccupied by the Israelites. The early settlement was clustered around a bamah, or cultic high place. The bamah became a royal Israelite sanctuary during the reign of Solomon (965-928 BCE), and was protected by a citadel. Five further Israelite citadels were built on the site between the ninth century BCE and the early sixth century BCE.

After the destruction of the last of the Israelite citadels at the end of the First Temple period (587-586 BCE), the site was abandoned. A brief occupation during the fifth century BCE led to some Persian building activity, though most of this was destroyed in the third to second century BCE when a large Hellenistic tower was built. The tower stood until the second century BCE.

The Romans built a fortress on the mound (c. 70-100 CE), possibly as part of the network of fortifications guarding the *Limes Palaestinae* (Dead Sea–Rafiah road). No remains were found on the tel from the Byzantine village mentioned in Eusebius' *Onomasticon*, though evidence suggests that the Roman fort was repaired and reoccupied during the Early Arab period (638-1099 CE). The mound was later used as a Muslim graveyard from the 10th to 16th centuries CE. The citadel has been rebuilt by archaeologists, with distinct sections from the tenth, ninth to eighth, and sixth centuries BCE, and the Hellenistic tower, clearly identifiable. Excavations and rebuilding continue at the site.

Tour of the site

The information leaflet provided has a map and an isometric reconstruction of the Canaanite city. A tour can begin at the top, at the Israelite citadel, which is accessible by car. However, you would still need to walk back up to collect your car. It is as well to begin at the bottom, chronologically, at the Canaanite city as the walk around is not very taxing.

Israelite citadel (Tel Hametzudot) The mound upon which the Israelite citadel stands rises above the lower (Canaanite) city to the southwest. The citadel that you see today has been largely rebuilt by the archaeologists who excavated the site, though they used the original materials. Six successive Israelite citadels stood on this site, plus later Persian, Hellenistic, Roman and Arab structures. Climbing to the observation point gives the best view of the citadel's plan, the Canaanite city below, and the surrounding countryside.

Though finds in the citadel area have revealed a hoard of silver ingots and jewellery, as well as evidence of a perfume industry, the most significant building within the citadel is the sanctuary, or temple. Its construction began in the Solomonic period (late 10th century BCE, though the bamah and altar predate it to the late 12th to early 11th centuries BCE. The temple is orientated east–west, like the Solomonic Temple in Jerusalem, and comprises three rooms: a hall, the sanctuary, and the holy of holies. A masseba, or ritual standing stone, was found in the holy of holies. The temple remained in use until the seventh century BCE, though the use of the sacrificial altar may have gone out of use during the religious reforms of Hezekiah (727-698 BCE). Currently excavators are at work digging out the remarkably deep water cisterns that lie below the citadel foundations.

Sacred Precinct The Sacred Precinct comprises a large twin temple, a small twin temple, and a large ceremonial structure, all within a self-contained complex separated from the other city buildings by a wall. The **large twin temple** to the west consists of two large halls identical in size, both opening on to courtyards. The northern hall is divided into three cells, and a large altar and a cult basin were found in its courtyard. The southern hall proved rich in finds, most notable of which is what is thought to be a *masseba*. The **small twin temple** in the centre of the Sacred Precinct is similar in plan. A number of finds were unearthed here, including a stone altar in the courtyard of the northern hall. The **ceremonial building** to the southeast comprises a large hall opening on to a wide courtyard. All the buildings in the Sacred Precinct open to the east, with the twin temples closely resembling the twin temples at Megiddo.

Palace complex The Palace complex was sealed off from the rest of the city buildings, with no doors or windows to the west, a main entrance to the north, and small doorways to the east and south. The location of the complex near to the Sacred Precinct was significant in determining its function as the governor's residence.

City walls and gates The **Canaanite city walls** extend for some 1200 m, enclosing an area of 10 ha. The wall is almost 2.5 m thick in most parts and is built of large, semi-dressed stones with a fill of smaller stones. The walls are reinforced by posterns, towers and gates, and being restored. The **western gate** was probably the main gate, suggested by its wide entrance, and is protected by a semicircular tower to its north.

Residential quarter The Canaanite city plan was well ordered, with a functional separation of districts. Typical dwelling units comprise a main room with benches running along the walls, a stone base for a wooden pillar to support the roof in the centre of the room, a smaller subsidiary room (a kitchen or storeroom), plus a courtyard. Such is the regularity of this building within the Canaanite city, such a broadhouse is now referred to as an **Aradian House**.

Water reservoir area It should be noted that the Canaanite city lacks a natural spring or well and is thus dependent upon collection and storage of rainwater. The Eocenic rock that the mound stands upon is different in character to the Senonian rock that surrounds it and, being impervious to water, it allows the storage of water in large cisterns.

At the lowest part of the city, the water reservoir area of the Canaanite city is a distinct complex of buildings surrounding the main reservoir on three sides. The largest building in the complex comprises five long, narrow chambers, with very thick outer walls and may well have been associated with the control and distribution of this most valuable of commodities

The plan of the original Canaanite city reservoir is not clear due to the later digging of the Israelite period well in the centre. The deep well, tapping the upper aquifer, supplied water that was carried in vessels to the cistern inside the Israelite citadel. The well was restored during the Herodian period, some time between 37 BCE and 70 CE.

Arad → *For listings, see pages 41-42.*

Though there are few attractions in Arad itself, the town is a good base for easy access to the west side of Masada, and is popular with Israeli walkers as many good treks can be had in the surrounding area. Arad is also worth visiting since it is one of the few development towns in the Negev that has been deemed to have worked. Arad lies close to the ancient Canaanite city at Tel Arad (see page 37), though its main claim to fame nowadays is as home to the renowned Israeli writer Amos Oz, and as the venue for the annual Hebrew Music Festival.

Arriving in Arad
Getting there and away There are four buses from Tel Aviv per day and frequent services from Be'er Sheva. Arriving from the direction of the Dead Sea, there are several buses per day from 'En Boqeq, Ein Gedi and Masada.

Getting around The town centre is very compact, though if you're heading out towards the eastern edge of town it is easier to hop on bus No 1 (which makes a long circuit all the way around the town).

Tourist information There is no longer a tourist information centre in Arad, but a decent map is available from the Inbar Hotel, and you can call Anna at the **Municipality** ⓘ *T08-9951622, Sun-Thu 1000-1530, for advice.*

Background

Earmarked as a Negev development town by the government in the early 1960s, the site for the new town was selected by a group of founding fathers. The layout of the town was developed by an interdisciplinary team who took into consideration physical, social, economic and demographic factors. Thus, there is a distinct separation of industrial, commercial and residential zones, with sufficient room for the town to expand in stages. Compared with other Negev development towns, Arad has been a success. As one long-time resident pointed out, "Those who planned towns such as Dimona never lived in them. The opposite is true of Arad" (Brook, *Winner Takes All*).

Arad is situated 600 m above sea level, at the point where the Judean Hills meet the Negev desert, and the views from this plateau are excellent. With a dry desert climate,

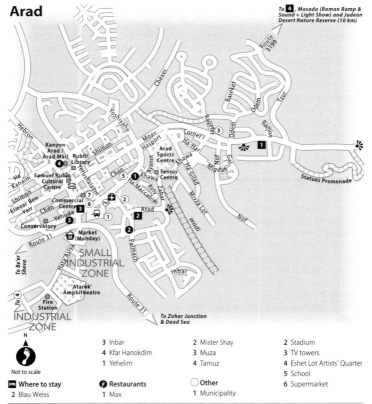

Arad

To **4**, Masada (Roman Ramp & Sound + Light Show) and Judean Desert Nature Reserve (10 km)

To Be'er Sheva

To **4**

SMALL INDUSTRIAL ZONE

INDUSTRIAL ZONE

To Zohar Junction & Dead Sea

N

Not to scale

■ **Where to stay**	❶ **Restaurants**	○ **Other**	
2 Blau Weiss	1 Max	1 Municipality	2 Stadium
3 Inbar	2 Mister Shay		3 TV towers
4 Kfar Hanokdim	3 Muza		4 Eshet Lot Artists' Quarter
1 Yehelim	4 Tamuz		5 School
			6 Supermarket

pollen-free air, and pollution-free environment, Arad has gained a reputation as a centre for the treatment of asthma and other respiratory problems.

Places in Arad
Eshet Lot Artists' Quarter Located by the western entrance to Arad, 2 km from town, the 'Lot's Wife' Artists' Quarter makes use of semi-derelict warehouses and hangars on the edge of the industrial area (a small-scale Mizpe Ramon, see page 63). The workshops and galleries tend to open only at weekends or by request, so be sure to call ahead before you visit. The **Glass Museum** ① *11 HaSadan, T08-9953388*, is a highlight, exhibiting the work of Gideon Friedman plus other glass artists, and there is a shop. Close by, at 9 HaSadan, is the **Earth and Clay Culture Museum** ① *T08-9939856*, where you can view installations, check out the ceramics gallery and browse the shop. The **Doll Museum** ① *14 HaSadan, T052-2398918*, is an extraordinary enterprise: the sculptor-owners show their works all over the world, created in porcelain, bronze and other materials (at times unsettlingly life-like). Unfortunately, entrance is only for groups, but call to see if there is a chance you can tag along.

Arad listings

For hotel and restaurant price codes and other relevant information, see pages 12-16.

Where to stay
Arad has a slim choice of hotels, though one is outstanding; package tourists will find themselves in one of the well-equipped hotels on the east side of town (not listed here).
$$$ Inbar, 38 Yehuda, T08-9973303, www.inbar-hotel.co.il. Rather unsightly block in centre of town, though rooms are pleasantly furnished in creams with pale wood, decent bathrooms, standard amenities and fairly priced, suites significantly larger. Heated indoor pool, salt water pool and dry sauna (outside guests 40NIS for day-use, call to check opening hrs), spa and mud treatments available in adjoining spa. Kosher restaurant.
$$$ Yehelim, 72 Moav, T077-2028120/6 or 052-6522718, www.yehelim.com, yehelim@gmail.com. One of the most charming boutique hotels in Israel, Yehelim's 10 rooms are secluded, some with balcony overlooking the desert hills, each has a unique layout but the same cool calm colour scheme, jacuzzi, wide beds, cute garden, beautiful terrace with Moroccan lamps. Standard rooms 600NIS, deluxe 720NIS (weekend price rise),

discounts for stays over 2 days. Wonderful breakfast included (outside guests welcome for breakfast, phone the day before), vegetarian/fish dinner available (guests only). Spa treatments available. Young children not allowed. Good advice on activities in the area. A peaceful haven on the eastern edge of town.
$$-$ Blau-Weiss Guest House and Youth Hostel, 4 Atad, T08-9957150, www.iyha.co.il. Clean a/c private chalets (doubles 336NIS during week) with TV and coffee corner, breakfast included, reception open 0800-1400, no curfew. Rooms sleep 2-5 people. Be sure to call in advance, they only open up when there are bookings.
$$-$ Kfar Hanokdim, T08-9950097, wwwkfarhanokdim.co.il. An oasis in the Judean desert, stunningly located in a valley between Arad and Masada (10 km away from each). Camel rides and a 'Bedouin experience' are encouraged as part of a stay, but you can just take a room, space in a tent or even pitch your own (they try to be accommodating and can provide sleeping bags). Cabins have personality, with Bedouin rugs everywhere, pretty coverlets, coral and driftwood decor, Hebron glass baubles, coffee corner. Great thought has gone into creating unique areas to relax outdoors,

with BBQs and lounging space. Bedouin hospitality includes music and chat about life before and life now. Meals in the attractive circular dining hall, with ludicrously large portions of traditional Bedouin dishes and a vast, delicious buffet breakfast. It's a good place to stay if you want to access Masada from the west, or are going to the Sound and Light show (see above).

Rooms for rent

There are several zimmers and "rooms for rent" in town, including Lavi's House, 13 Irit, T08-9954791 and Villa 1000, T08-9954423.

Restaurants and bars

There are no really outstanding restaurants in Arad. There are plenty of cafés, pizza parlours and kebab places in the Commercial Centre, plus a big supermarket nearby in the Kanyon Mall. For a special breakfast, call the Yehelim (see Where to stay, above).

$$ Max, T08-9973339. Mon-Wed 1800-2400, Thu 1800-0200, Fri 1800-0300, Sat 1200-0100. This shack-like building in a rather derelict park morphs into a lively evening drinking and dining spot, with good music and a better atmosphere. Some outside tables.

$$ Mister Shay, 32 Palmach, T08-9971956. Mon-Sat 1200-2300. Serves a large spread of Chinese food and cheap (for Israel) sushi, plus the odd Thai dish. Plenty of veg options (though rather mundane), meat eaters will be spoilt for choice, set menus for 2 from 169NIS, business lunch 40-60NIS. Tastefully and brightly decorated in Asian colours. Wireless available. The restaurant is behind a grocery shop, down some steps.

$$ Muza, T08-9958764. (Only closes between 0600-0800 each day for cleaning!) The liveliest pub in town is definitely Muza, weirdly located behind the Alon petrol station on the western entrance to Arad. The interior is coated with football colours and license plates, with a 'real' bar and screens for watching sport. Great outdoor area, large menu of Israeli-Western food and lots of imported beers. Ask about the food/drink deals. Shabbat is raucous.

$$ Tamuz, in the Kanyon Arad Mall. Dairy restaurant/café with a mixed menu of light meals and salads. Recommended.

Festivals

The population of Arad used to double during the annual **Hebrew Music Festival** (Festival Arad). After a long spell of absence, the festival was back in 2009, held during Sukkot (Sep/Oct). To get the latest information call the Municipality on T106.

Shopping

The main shopping area is the **Kanyon Arad** (Arad Mall) and the nearby **Commercial Centre** between Eliezar Ben Yair and Yehuda. **Arad Market** takes place each Mon. A branch of **Steimatzsky** in the mall sells the Jerusalem Post, but has poor fiction/travel selection.

Transport
Bus

Arad's 'Bus Station' is on Yehuda. **Be'er Sheva**, bus 388, Sun-Thu frequent service from 0530-2200, Fri until 1646, Sat from 1800, 1 hr. **Dead Sea destinations**, bus 384/385 Sun-Thu 0705 1015 1300 1545, Fri 1030 1335. **Tel Aviv** 389 direct, Sun-Thu 4 buses per day, 0600 0830 1600 1900, Fri last at 1330, Sat 1800 2100, 1½ hrs, 39NIS. **Jerusalem** 554, Sun-Thu 0730 1430 1700, Fri 1100 1345, Sat 2130 2200, 3 hrs. The best option for **Eilat** is to change at Be'er Sheva. For **Tel Arad**, take one of the buses bound for **Be'er Sheva** or **Tel Aviv** and ask to be dropped at the Tel Arad Junction (2.5-km walk to the site).

Dimona → *For listings, see page 43.*

Whilst Arad is often held up as a model for the Negev development towns, Dimona is frequently selected by commentators as the example of the one that didn't work. From modest beginnings in 1955, the population has increased to around 40,000, a sizeable proportion of whom are Jews of North African origin, plus a more recent Russian influx. The economy of the town has traditionally been sustained by four major industries, despite the fact that the remoteness of the location increases transport costs considerably. Severe staff cut-backs at the textile factories, the chemical factory, and to a certain extent at the Dead Sea Works, led to high levels of unemployment in the early 1990s though the situation has improved in recent years.

Dimona's other major 'business', sometimes euphemistically referred to as the 'chocolate factory', is the country's leading **nuclear research station**. The facility is located off the road 13 km east of the town, though sightseers are not encouraged. It's not even recommended that you stop to take a look and don't even think about getting your camera out. When a former employee at the site, **Mordechai Vanunu**, spilled the beans about Israel's nuclear capacity to the London *Sunday Times*, he was lured to Rome by a female Mossad agent, kidnapped, and brought back to Israel to stand trial. After serving 18 years in jail he was released in 2004, though his movements and speech are severely restricted (he cannot leave Israel nor talk to foreign press).

Dimona's other main talking point is the presence of the 2000-strong community of African Hebrew Israelites, popularly referred to as the **Black Hebrews**. The group have established their own 'village of peace' within Dimona, and the community welcomes visitors who take a genuine interest in their beliefs and the way that they live. It is advisable to phone ahead (call **Yafah** ① *T052-3910858*, at least 24 hours in advance) and someone will show you around. Community shops cover a diverse range of activities, from the Sisterhood Boutique selling their unique style of clothing made of 100% natural fabrics, the grocery store selling organic and vegan products, to the specialist hair-braiding salon (by appointment only). The two-day New World Passover in late May celebrates the Exodus from America, with dance, sporting events and family activities, and attracts a few hundred foreign visitors. Their compound is on Herzl, 10 minutes' walk from the bus station.

Dimona listings

For hotel and restaurant price codes and other relevant information, see pages 12-16.

Where to stay and restaurants
$$-$ Black Hebrews' Guesthouse, T08-6555400. Open Sun-Thu 1030-2100, Fri 0830-1400. Advance booking essential. Simple rooms, price includes half-board. Visitors are asked to respect their regulations, which means no cigarettes, alcohol or meat products to be brought into the community. Guests have access (for a small fee) to small gym, sauna, jacuzzi and exercise classes. Easily the best (and cheapest) place in town to eat is at the Black Hebrews' vegan café, which has lunch and dinner specials (eg casserole), as well as sandwiches, raw foods and tofu dishes. The (soya) ice cream is popular: flavour changes daily. The community also runs the Taste of Life vegan café in Tel Aviv .

The large mall on the opposite side of Road 25 from the town centre has a branch of Aroma, which is always reliable for generously sized and tasty salads, sandwiches and the like.

Transport
Bus
Be'er Sheva, buses 48/56, 2 per hr, 30-45 mins, 11NIS; **Eilat**, buses 393/394/397,

Sun-Thu 0755-0150, Fri 0755-1800, Sat 1805-0150, 3 hrs; **Tel Aviv**, buses 393/394, every hr or so Sun-Thu 0740-2140, Fri 0740-1740, Sat 1410-2140, 2 hrs 45 mins.

Mamshit → *For listings, see page 47.*

① *T08-6556478. Daily 0800-1700 (winter 0800-1600), closes 1 hr earlier on Fri and hol eves. Adult 21NIS, student 17NIS, child 9NIS. Mamshit is 6 km southeast of Dimona along Route 25. The Dimona–Eilat bus (395/397) stops at the turning for the site, from where it is 1.5 km along the side road.*

During the reign of their King Obodas III (c. 28 BCE-9 CE), the Nabateans established a number of large settlements in the Negev, ostensibly as way stations on the network of roads that comprised the Spice Road between their Edom capital at Petra and the Mediterranean Sea at Gaza. The extensive remains commonly referred to by the Hebrew name Mamshit (the Arabic name Kurnub sounds better to the English ear) are the site of one such Nabatean city. Mamshit was important enough to feature on the Madaba Map, and you get a good sense of this past as you walk through rooms and turn corners of clearly defined streets in the ancient city.

Background

Early Roman/Middle Nabatean period A town was probably established here during the reign of the Nabatean king Obodas III, in the Early Roman period (also known as the Middle Nabatean period, 37 BCE-132 CE). Roads almost certainly connected Mamshit to other Nabatean towns, most notably Gaza via Oboda (Hebrew: Avdat), though it should be noted that Mamshit was on a secondary and not the main trade route. Its status and prosperity may well have increased in the Late Nabatean period when Roman engineers cut steps forming the Ma'ale Aqrabim (or Scorpions' Ascent, see page 49) to the southeast, on the road to Petra.

Much of the Nabatean kingdom was annexed by the Roman Empire in 106 CE, though this is not considered to have lessened the general prosperity of the Negev. The Nabateans had begun to establish a sophisticated system of agriculture in the central Negev, cultivating the desert by collecting rainwater in carefully constructed terraces in the narrow valleys. Potential arable land at Mamshit was scarce, however, and thus much of the town's economy was based upon the rearing of racehorses. This lack of arable land may also explain why Mamshit, with a population of around 1000, is considerably smaller than Nessana (Nizzana, population 4000) and Oboda (Avdat, population 3000).

Middle and Late Roman/Late Nabatean period One of the key features of Nabatean towns is the quality of the architecture, and Mamshit is no exception. Initially, the towns featured the characteristic Nabatean large public buildings, with only the army living in permanent quarters and most of the population living in tents. The Late Nabatean period saw a new town plan laid out, initiated largely by the construction of upper-class housing, and with the main north–south axis now dividing public buildings from the residential areas. The Nabateans used their knowledge and mastery of constructing grand building designs, and adapted it to their domestic architecture. The Middle and Late Roman periods (Late Nabatean period) saw the construction of large, spacious houses around a central courtyard, sometimes up to three storeys high. The homes were designed to be cool in summer and warm in winter. Many of the sizeable Nabatean buildings seen at the site today date to the Late Nabatean period.

During the Late Roman period, Mamshit was integrated within the southern defence system of the Roman Empire, probably guarding the Jerusalem–Aila (Eilat) road, and a fortified wall was built around the settlement. It appears that the Romans made few additions to the built environment, instead taking advantage of the high-quality building techniques of the Nabateans. It is interesting to note that much of the town's economy became based upon the payment of salaries from the imperial treasury to resident soldiers. When the Eternal Peace agreement was concluded by the Emperor Justinian in 561 CE and the military payments ceased, the economy of Mamshit went into severe decline.

Byzantine period The major change at Mamshit during the Byzantine period (324-638 CE) was that most of the population turned from paganism to Christianity. Two of Mamshit's most prominent buildings, the Eastern Church and the Western Church, date to this period. A number of buildings were destroyed by a strong earthquake in 363 CE. Mamshit was probably destroyed by local Arab tribesmen prior to the full-scale occupation of the Negev by the Arabs in 636 CE.

Tour of the site
The following tour proceeds in a roughly anti-clockwise direction from the entrance. An information leaflet, with map, is provided, plus there are useful boards around the site with diagrammatic reconstructions of how the buildings would have appeared. The text below is intended to complement rather than repeat the information given at the site.

Nabatean caravanserai These large buildings standing outside the later city walls served as inns and remained buried by deep sand dunes for a long period of time. They are missing from the plan of the site that T E Lawrence (Lawrence of Arabia) helped prepare in 1914.

Main city gate The city's main gate was defended by two unequally sized towers, later expanded, and closed by sturdy wooden doors. Remains of the burnt doors were found in the debris of the gate. It is interesting to note that the main gate is not aligned with the main street of the Late Nabatean town.

Late Roman city walls Most Nabatean settlements were unwalled, relying instead for their defence on a series of strategically placed towers within the town itself. When the Romans absorbed the central Negev area within the southern defence system of their empire, Mamshit's compact size meant that it could be encircled by a defensive wall. The walls run for just under 1 km, taking advantage of the contours of the land and taking into account existing buildings. They are reinforced by a number of towers.

Water-supply system Accomplished engineers as well as architects and masons, the Nabateans thrived in their desert environment through their ability to construct complex, but reliable, water-supply systems. Mamshit's water was controlled by three dams on Nahal Mamshit, a water-conservation system built above the high waterfall of a tributary of the Nahal Mamshit, plus several water-retaining pools engineered to the south and west. A small Water Gate was added to the western wall in the Late Roman period to allow water to be brought into the town from the three dams on the Nahal Mamshit.

Mansion The large (35 m by 20 m) building to the northeast of the tower may have been the mansion of a city official during the Late Nabatean period. The complex features a guardroom, guest quarters and offices, with the main residential area on the upper balconied storey.

Watchtower A good view of the entire city and the ancient dam in Nahal Mamshit can be had from the top of the tower, which is 5 m high. The square tower adjoins a courtyard containing a large reservoir. The tower may have served as a combined observation tower/administrative centre during the Middle and Late Nabatean periods.

Western Church The more elaborate of Mamshit's two churches in its execution, the Western Church has been well restored. The nave mosaic depicts birds, fruit, swastikas and flowers on a geometric pattern, with a central inscription within a medallion reading: "Lord, Help your servant Nilus, the builder of this place, Amen." The Western Church was destroyed in a violent conflagration. Dating the church has been problematic, with the mosaic inscriptions providing no clues. A coin found in the upper levels of the church foundations belongs to the reign of the Roman Emperor Probus (276-282 CE), whilst another coin found amongst the fill of the foundation pit dates to the late fourth century CE. Behind the church is a typical Nabatean house, with stables for 16 horses.

Eastern Church The plan of the Byzantine Eastern Church is almost identical to that of the Western Church. It is also notable for its high standard of workmanship and, unusually for a Byzantine period building, the construction methods are Roman. Dating the church precisely has not been possible, though certain clues have enabled experts to make an educated guess. The geometric mosaic pavement in the nave has two crosses incorporated into the design. Since the practice of depicting the cross on a church floor was banned in 427 CE, it is concluded that the church must predate this decree. Further, coins dating to the reigns of the Eastern Roman Emperors Diocletian (284-305 CE, in the pre-church era) and Theodosius I (379-395 CE) were discovered in the foundations, suggesting the church was built some time during the latter's reign. Part of a monastery complex, an adjacent courtyard (atrium) contains a deep cistern. Small reliquaries sunk into the floor next to the altar, and a simple grave in a side room, contain the bones of supposed saints or martyrs.

Market area The market area comprises three rows of shops lining two streets. (It is roofed with palm leaves for when a present-day 'Nabatean Market' is staged, during both Pesach and Sukkot).

British police station This relatively modern building is the former headquarters of the Negev desert police (who were mounted on camels) during the British Mandate period. The construction of the police station destroyed much of what may have been the Middle Nabatean fortress building. There are good views from the top (and also from behind) down Wadi Mamshit.

'Nabatu' House One of the finest examples of the ability of Late Nabatean architects, the complex features a central courtyard with columns topped by well-formed capitals, standing on a stylobate. Stables lead off from the courtyard, each horse having a stone trough and arched stone window to their stall. The treasure room stood to the south of the courtyard, and is identifiable by the frescoes on the arches and upper walls of its vestibule. A hoard of 10,500 silver dinars and tetradrachms was found in a bronze jar concealed beneath the ruins of a staircase. The oldest of the coins date to the reign of the Nabatean King Rabbel II (70-106 CE), with the latest dating to the rule of the Roman Emperor Elagabalus (218-222 CE).

Bathhouse Dating of the bathhouse is uncertain; it was certainly in use during the Byzantine period, though it may actually have been built during the Late Nabatean period. The entrance leads to a central courtyard lined with stone benches, which probably served as the changing room. The cold room (*frigidarium*) has two sitting baths. A connecting door leads to the *tepidarium*, or lukewarm room, with the hot baths comprising three rooms (*caldarium*) sunk into the ground. Remains of the plumbing system that brought water and took away the waste can also be seen. To the east of the bathhouse, adjacent to the city walls, is a large public pool that was used as a reservoir, supplied by water carried by man and beast from the wadi to the west of the town.

Cemeteries Though not enclosed within the Mamshit National Park area (nor shown on the site map), three main cemeteries associated with the site have been excavated; the main Nabatean necropolis 1 km to the north of the city, a Roman cemetery 200 m to the northeast, and a Byzantine cemetery 500 m to the west of the city.

Mamshit listings

For hotel and restaurant price codes and other relevant information, see pages 12-16.

Where to stay and restaurants
$$-$ Negev Camel Ranch, T08-6552829, www.cameland.co.il. 12 huts, simple yet comfortable, decorated with plain coloured mats and desert colours. Heater, a/c, Bedouin seating inside and out. Dorm-style 100NIS, or US$56 per couple for a private hut, plus 20NIS per extra person. Bear in mind this is the desert, and dung beetles and lizards are visitors, plus a tribe of dogs and 40 female camels are near neighbours! Deliciously wholesome vegetarian "camel herder's supper": rice, lentils, veg stew, salad, bread baked on a hot stone, dates and tea to follow (adult/child US$14/12). Great breakfast (adult/child US$9/6). Beer and soft drinks available, making it a good place to come and hang out wherever you are staying. Good clean bathrooms and kitchen for guests use. Pick up from Dimona not a problem, or the Eliat bus passes nearby. Recommended.
$ Mamshit Campsite, cheap at 65NIS a dorm bed, but this could mean sharing with 200 people and all you get is a mattress. However, if one of the Tukuls (little huts with rush roofs and rug-interior walls) is free you will be given a place here (sleeps 5-6) or you can use your own tent for 50NIS per person. Bear in mind it's geared towards school groups. Kitchen facilities, and decent shower/toilet block.

What to do
Negev Camel Ranch, see above, provides a great opportunity to take a camel safari into the desert. Rides go on the hour every day, no minimum number and no advance arrangement required (unless you are a large group). A scenic hour's ride will pass near the ruins of Mamshit and along the cliffs above the wadi (adult/child 65/55NIS). There are also 2-hr and 4-hr trips, or you can book a 2-day safari including all equipment and food. Owner Ariel (and his staff) provide good information and advice on local trekking and biking, given free of charge. Anyone is welcome to drop by and it's recommended to do so before a trip, as desert conditions can be so changeable. You can pay to have someone drop you off/pick you up at the start/finish of hikes, and there

is overnight accommodation, see above. The ranch is 6 km southeast of Dimona, down the same road as Mamshit. 200 m from the main Route 25, a track branches left to the ranch.

Makhtesh HaGadol and Makhtesh HaKatan (craters)

Lying to the southeast of Be'er Sheva are two impressive erosion craters, formed by the same geological process as the Negev's more famous erosion crater, Makhtesh Ramon (see page 69). In fact, the Makhtesh HaKatan (small crater) is the most visually stunning as it can be seen in its entirety and thus the impact is more striking. There are several excellent hikes that can be made in the Makhtesh HaGadol (Great Makhtesh) and Makhtesh HaKatan area, as well as a number of archaeological remains which add interest, though many visitors just drive through and admire the views.

Arriving in Makhtesh HaGadol and Makhtesh HaKatan
Getting there and away Unfortunately, the sites and hiking trail heads described below are not accessible by public transport, and as none of the hikes is circular, you will need transport waiting at the finishing points or make an arrangement for pick-up/drop-off with your guesthouse.

The Makhtesh HaGadol, Makhtesh HaKatan

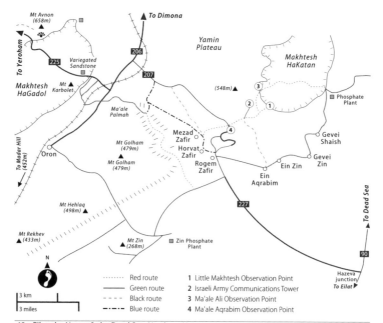

········ Red route	1 Little Makhtesh Observation Point
—— Green route	2 Israeli Army Communications Tower
– – – Black route	3 Ma'ale Ali Observation Point
–·–·– Blue route	4 Ma'ale Aqrabim Observation Point

There are several points of access to the two craters. They can be approached from the northwest via Yeroham (a Negev development town 13 km southwest of Dimona); from the north, via Rotem Junction where Route 25 meets the 204; and from the southeast, from Hazeva Junction at the meeting point of Route 90 (The Arava Road) and Route 227.

Note The usual rules about hiking in the desert apply. The map here is for information only, and should be complemented with the relevant sheets of the SPNI 1:50,000 map. The words 'wadi' and 'nahal' (river) are used interchangeably below.

Visiting Makhtesh HaGadol and Makhtesh HaKatan

Ma'ale 'Aqrabim hike (Scorpion's Ascent) The starting point for this strenuous six- to seven-hour hike is the Rogem Zafir (the starting or finishing point for a number of walks, most of which are marked on the signboard and map). The larger of the two structures comprising Rogem Zafir is a fort, formerly two storeys high. A number of coins were found here, mostly depicting the images of Roman emperors and dating from the third and fourth centuries CE. The two structures served as a staging post on the Petra–Gaza Spice Road.

The route described here runs in a southeast to northwest direction. It follows blue trail markers for most of its journey, with a number of diversions and extensions marked in green and black. It is entirely feasible to do the walk in reverse, of course, thus descending more than ascending and enjoying the view spread out in front of you.

The route incorporates the Ma'ale 'Aqrabim, or Scorpions' Ascent, part of an ancient route linking the northern Arava with the northern Negev Hills. This area featured heavily in the wanderings of Moses and the Children of Israel, though his followers were not impressed: "And why have ye brought up the congregation of the Lord into this wilderness, that we and our cattle should die there?" (*Numbers 20:4*). This area was later described to Moses by God as the southern border of the land that the Jews should settle: "And your border shall turn from the south to the ascent of Akrabbim, and pass on to Zin ..." (*Numbers 34:4*).

The turning point in the fortunes of this route was when the Roman engineers cut a cliff road into the steep escarpment during the Late Roman period (132-324 CE). Whereas the average slope of the natural escarpment was 34°, and thus unsuitable for pack animals, the sharp curves and terraced steps that the Romans constructed reduced this gradient to a manageable 16°. As you climb up, you may wish that the Romans had reduced the gradient by a bit more. The staircase was largely rebuilt during the British Mandate period.

There is a shorter, but steeper, path off to the right, leading to the Ma'ale 'Aqrabim Observation Point, though the route described here continues in a northwest direction, between two wadis, before you encounter the first staircase. Five flights of stairs later, you arrive at the top of the Roman **Ma'ale 'Aqrabim**. The building remains here are Horvat Zafir, a Roman fortress that guarded the route. About 500 m to the south are the remains of an ancient dam.

The blue trail continues north, in the direction of the remains of the fort on the top of the hill about 1.5 km in front of you. This is Mezad Zafir, another square Roman fort. From Mezad Zafir there are several options. The red trail leads east, towards the **Ma'ale Ali Observation Point** and the **Little Makhtesh Observation Point**, intersecting the main road, Route 227, on the way (see map). The black trail heads northwest, rejoining Route 227 after about 4.5 km. The blue trail continues west-north-west, after 4.5 km either following the Ma'ale Yamin (Yamin ascent) back to Route 227, or allowing a diversion for a further 6 km along the green route of the Big Fin trail back to the **Variegated Sandstone** (some beautiful sandstone formations featuring a bold display of yellows, ochres, reds and purples).

Southern Negev

This Southern Negev section principally follows the 220-km journey south from Be'er Sheva via Mizpe Ramon to Eilat. Notable sights en route include the Ein Avdat Nature Reserve, the Nabatean city of Avdat (Oboda), the Negev's most spectacular natural feature, the Makhtesh Ramon, as well as the resort city of Eilat itself. In addition to the sights on the main Route 40 (all accessible by public transport), there are a number of excursions to sights off this road, most of which require you to have your own transport.

Haluza (Elusa)

Haluza is the Nabatean settlement of Elusa, established as part of the Petra–Oboda–Gaza Spice Road some time in the third century BCE. Because of its remote location, Elusa receives few visitors and hence the presentation is not up to much. Most of the site is covered by wind-blown sand and dust; pretty much as it was when Robinson discovered and identified it in 1838, and Woolley and Lawrence (of Arabia) described it in 1914. The most substantial remains are the theatre and the east church, located close together on the southeast side of the site.

Arriving in Haluza (Elusa)
Getting there and away Haluza is located southwest of Be'er Sheva, although you need to head south of Be'er Sheva along Route 40 for 30 km to Mash'abbe Sade Junction, then head northwest along Route 222 for 20 km to reach the site. See 'Be'er Sheva to Mizpe Ramon' map, page 34, for orientation. You really need your own transport to reach Haluza, although bus 45 from Be'er Sheva to Kibbutz Revivim runs eight times per day (continuing northwest along Route 222).

Background
The principal Nabatean finds from the site date to the reigns of the Nabatean kings Aretas I (c. 168 BCE) and Aretas IV (c. 9 BCE-40 CE). However, it was during the Late Nabatean and Late Roman periods that Elusa reached its peak, eventually becoming the major Byzantine city in the Negev.

There are numerous written references to Elusa, providing some insight into the city's history. Ptolemy refers to Elusa, as does the writer Libanius in two mid-fourth century CE letters. Elusa is also listed on the Roman cartographer Castorius' 'road atlas' of the Roman Empire, *Tabula Peutingeriana* (c. 365 CE). Christian references to Elusa, however, are more problematic. The assertion by both Jerome and Nilus that Christians and idolaters lived side by side in Elusa during the early fifth century cannot be proven since the earliest Christian epitaph thus found at the site dates to 519 CE. There are also important references to Elusa in the Nessana Papyri (see box, page 53).

The site
The **theatre** was first constructed in the Middle Nabatean period, in the first half of the first century CE. Later additions were made, and it seems to have remained in use until the middle of the Byzantine period at least. The cavea, or spectators' seating area, is about 35 m in diameter, though it is not well preserved. The 'VIP' box in the centre is still discernible, however. The *orchestra* area in front of the stage is quite well preserved, though inscriptions suggest that a new floor was laid as recently as 455 CE. The Nabatean theatre at Elusa had cultic uses, with the site's excavators believing that a Nabatean temple stood nearby.

Part of the reason that the east church was excavated so thoroughly was because it was thought that it may stand on the site of the Nabatean temple connected with the theatre. Because of this attention paid to the east church, it is probably the most impressive attraction at Elusa today. The church is particularly large (27 m by 77 m), with many limestone columns and Proconessian marble Corinthian capitals still *in situ*. The base of a bishop's throne has been identified within the central apse, suggesting that the church was in fact the region's cathedral. It has not been possible to date the church conclusively, though the building style is comparable with other churches built in the Negev between 350 CE and 450 CE.

Shivta (Sobata)

ⓘ *Open all hours. Admission free.*
Though not part of the main Petra–Oboda–Gaza Spice Road, the Nabatean town of Sobata (Arabic: Subeita) was still linked to Oboda (Avdat) and Nessana (Nizzana) by road. The principal points of interest are the churches, though parts of the Nabatean and Byzantine towns remain. Because of its remoteness, Shivta receives few visitors and entrance is still free. This, however, may soon change as the site is scheduled for restoration. Visit now, while Shivta retains its magical and isolated aura. There is a Nabatean restaurant and charming small guesthouse near the entrance.

Arriving in Shivta (Sobata)
Getting there and away From Tlalim Junction on Route 40, head southwest for 20 km, then turn south for 8 km to the site (passing a number of burnt-out Egyptian tanks from the 1948 war). Metropoline bus 44 passes the turn-off, but hitching the last 8 km would be difficult, especially as the bus leaves Be'er Sheva Sunday to Thursday at 1900 and Friday at 1400.

Background
Sobata was probably founded during the time of the Nabatean king Aretas IV (c. 9 BCE-40 CE), or perhaps during the reign of his predecessor Obodas III (c. 28-9 BCE). The Romans seem to have had little impact upon Sobata, probably not even stationing a garrison and not fortifying the town. Sobata increased in importance during the Byzantine period (324-638 CE), possibly becoming a centre of Christian scholarship and pilgrimage. The Nessana Papyri (see box, page 53) again suggest no permanent military presence during this period, though there are plenty of references to the agricultural economy.

There is evidence to suggest that following the Arab conquest of the region (636 CE), Christians and Muslims lived in peace together here. As one of the site's chief excavators, Avraham Negev, points out, the builders of the mosque were at pains not to damage the adjoining baptistry of the South Church.

Places in Shivta (Sobata)

The **North Church** was probably built in two separate phases, beginning life as a single apsidal basilica in the middle of the fourth century CE. Considerable additions were made in the first half of the sixth century CE to make the church triapsidal. The church is attended by a monastery, a chapel, a baptistry and a mortuary chapel.

The **South Church** is smaller, constrained in its construction by the positioning of the double reservoir on its west side. For this reason there is no *atrium* (entrance forecourt), an unusual feature considering that the contemporary churches at Elusa, Rehovot-in-the-Negev, and the North Church here all have particularly large atriums. The apses were previously plastered and painted, with one such scene depicting the Transfiguration of Jesus, though it is hard to make out the subject of the paintings today. The well-preserved baptistry to the north of the church is adjoined by a small mosque.

Nizzana (Nessana)

① *Open 24 hours. Admission free.*

Route 211 from Shivta continues west to one of the least populated regions in the country, where about 120 families live in five tiny villages. Groups of trees along this road signal where the Turkish built their 'Li'man': way stations for travellers, with dams to collect run-off water and trees to give shade. Nizzana is the site of the Nabatean Spice Road town of Nessana, and is famed as the place where the so-called Nessana Papyri were found (see box, page 53). The mound that Nessana stands upon looks impressive and mystical from a distance, though closer inspection reveals that many significant archaeological remains have been lost. The construction of the North Church in the Byzantine period obscured many of the Nabatean buildings, perhaps including the main Nabatean temple. Further, the use of the site by the Turkish administration early in the 20th century, including the 'recycling' of building material for construction of buildings throughout the area, destroyed many of the older remains.

Arriving in Nizzana (Nessana)

Getting there and away Nizzana lies around 20 km further west along Route 211 from the turning for Shivta (see 'Be'er Sheva to Mizpe Ramon' map, page 34, for orientation). Metropoline bus 44 goes to Ezuz Sunday to Thursday at 1900, Friday at 1400, returning the next day at 0600, passing Nizzana on the way.

Background

The Byzantine period (324-638 CE) was the period of Nessana's greatest prosperity, with the settlement expanding significantly and the major buildings at the site today dating from this period. The significant Nessana Papyri also date to this period, between the sixth and late seventh centuries CE (see box, page 53). Though there was a smooth transition to Arab rule in the seventh century CE, there are no remains at Nessana (Arabic: 'Auja el-Hafir) suggesting occupation later than the eighth century CE. With no evidence of a conflagration or a violent end, it is suggested that the agricultural land that supported the settlement fell into disuse, thus accelerating the city's decline.

Places in Nizzana (Nessana)

The **Roman fortress**, probably built in the first half of the fourth century CE (though this date is disputed), occupies much of the mound to the south of the North Church. There

The Nessana Papyri

During excavations at Nessana undertaken by the British School of Archaeology in Jerusalem, a significant discovery was made in a small room in the North Church: the Nessana Papyri. Written in Greek and bilingual Greek-Arabic, the papyri cover a number of subjects from the literary and theological to military, administrative and petty legal matters, all dating from the period of the sixth to late seventh century CE.

Though the literary and theological documents are important, and include several chapters of the Gospel of St John, details of the exploits and martyrdom of Saint George, plus a Greek dictionary accompanying Virgil's Aeneas, the nonliterary documents are particularly significant for the information that they provide on the economic, social and military life of the central Negev region during the period 512 CE to 689 CE.

Amongst the subjects discussed are marriage, divorce, inheritance, plus various bills of sale and financial contracts. There are also important references to wheat and grain yields, taxes, and payments of monthly salaries to the militias stationed at places such as Oboda and Mamshit, thus allowing a partial reconstruction of the socio-political administration of the region.

are a series of rooms along the long (85-m) west and east walls, though the rooms on the east side are thought to have been added later. The fortress is defended by a number of towers, with the main gate in the south tower and a secondary entrance in the east tower. The long monumental staircase up to the mound is now thought to date to the second half of the first century BCE, and not the Byzantine period as initially thought, and thus is assumed to have led to a Nabatean temple and not the fortress.

Dating the North Church is not precise, though two burials within the church have epigraphic references mentioning the dates 464 CE and 474 CE. Remains of three saints were found in a marble reliquary in one of the rooms, with inscriptions within the church dedicating it to the saints Sergius and Bacchus (with a mention of St Stephen). The Southern Court opens into the mono-apsidal basilica. To the west of the basilica is a baptistry, though at some stage parts of the east end were removed in order to make the basilica longer. Other later additions, including the North Court and the covered gallery date to the reign of the (East) Byzantine Emperor Justinian (527-565 CE).

On a separate mound some 60 m southwest of the fortress is the South Church. An inscription dates the church to 601-602 CE, and dedicates it to the Virgin Mary. The three-apse style was a feature of churches in this region.

Ezuz → *For listings, see page 54.*

Some of the stones pilfered from Nizzana can be seen in the constructions along the narrow road south to Ezuz. The Turks built a railway line down this route, across the desert to Egypt, and the old railway station can be seen to the left of the road. At the end of the road is Ezuz, formed in 1985 (and not officially recognized by the Israeli government) where 13 families live. Right on the border with Egypt, it is definitely Israel's Wild West. The reason it is so desolate is that the area is largely a fire zone, which preserves the natural environment but also means you can't do much trekking or biking (except at weekends). On the edge of the village, a Turkish railway bridge remains in its original form, and a 'bustan' (garden) has a remarkable well. Deep rope-marks have been worn into the sides where the water was brought up, before being poured into channels to water the camels. It was also channelled via an aqueduct to a large Byzantine pool in the wadi, and then used for agriculture. Leaving Ezuz, it's possible to drive down Route 10 (only during daylight and with the permission of the army, which may not be given due to recent security threats), to Mitzpe: an interesting, untravelled road. **Note** The nearest petrol station is 55 km away at Tlalim Junction.

Ezuz listings

For hotel and restaurant price codes and other relevant information, see pages 12-16.

Where to stay and restaurants
$$$ Zimmer Bus, Ezuz. Truly unique accommodation in 3 old buses, which have been clad in adobe and beautifully converted into comfortable and cool 'apartments', decorated with mosaics and coloured glass, Don't think motorhome – these are very desres. Two are perfect for families (playroom for kids in driver's compartment, a/c, fully self-catering), other suits a couple (no kitchen but can order meals). No TVs in sight.
$$$-$$ Beer Otayim, near Ezuz, T08-6555788, www.beerotayim.co.il. A very special place. Remote, rustic, desert chic. The rush-walled dining room is made from all natural materials; mud-clad rooms have mat, mattresses and stoves (no need for locks on the palm-wood doors); hammocks and wicker seats for chilling, and a central campfire. But it's the bathrooms that will wow you, with Armenian ceramic basins facing the empty desert. No guest kitchen facilities but excellent food provided, solar power, oil-lamps, eco-conscious. In one of 16 rooms: singles/couples 270/490NIS half-board, or 150NIS per person without food. Desert sounds include crickets, donkeys and the occasional crump of an explosion at the distant firing range! You're sure to meet interesting people, if only the staff. Book in advance; they will pick up from bus stop. Guests get cheap rates for camel trips. Follow the road to Ezuz from Nizzana, after about 15 km the road forks, turn right then right again (following the camel sign), the khan is 800 m along the wadi (tricky to find in the dark).

$$-$ Café, Ezuz, T054-4226330. Creating a Sinai beach-vibe in the depths of the desert, this little coffee shop specializes in crêpes (owner Eyal is French), has excellent pizza, shakshuka, cous-cous, soups, and ice cream in summer. It's basically a palm-leaf hut, with seating scattered about. Sometimes live jazz/blues at the weekend, or there's a LP collection to choose from. Booze available, good sunset spot. Open weekends and holidays from breakfast till late, otherwise phone in advance. Eyal also has a simple little hut for rent, windows all round, cosy and colourful, porch with view, outside kitchen and bathroom, compost toilet, suitable for couples (B&B, mid-week 300NIS, weekend 400NIS).

What to do
Camel safaris
Beer Otayim, www.beerotayim.co.il. Trips from 1½ hrs (adult/child 80/60NIS: 10NIS discount for guests at the khan), 3 hrs with a stop for tea, or 5 hrs with lunch. Guides are informative, and tailor trips to your interests, be it geology (fossils), history (rock art), flora (medicinal plants), or politics (the border). Cheaper rates for guests at the khan. Longer safaris, up to 10 days, also possible, eg for a group of 10 it would be 350NIS per person per day.

Cycling
There's a great single-track route marked out around Ezuz, though you need your own mountain bike.

Sde Boker → *For listings, see pages 57-58.*

Kibbutz Sde Boker is best known today for its association with Israel's first Prime Minister, David Ben-Gurion, who unexpectedly retired from politics in 1953 choosing instead to settle on the fledgling kibbutz. However, it is the phenomenally beautiful scenery, good hiking and excellent mountain biking that is most appreciated by foreign visitors. Midreshet Sde Boker, 3 km south of the kibbutz, is a great base for treks into the 'Wilderness of Zin'. Here you can find good accommodation, bicycle hire, and easy access to the beautiful Nahal Zin Nature Trail through the Ein Avdat National Park. There is an excellent (unique!) topographical map in English for the area showing biking, hiking and 4x4 trails, scale 1:50,000, which makes it easier to strike out into the desert.

Arriving in Sde Boker

Getting there and away Sde Boker is on the main Route 40, Egged buses 392 from Be'er Sheva to Eilat stop at the kibbutz and then at the Midreshet, four to six buses per day, first 0815, last 1545 (but check www.egged.co.il). Metropoline bus 60 between Be'er Sheva and Mizpe Ramon also stops here (about one per hour).

Tourist information Anyone attempting to hike in the region (excepting the simple Nahal Zin Nature Trail in Ein Avdat National Park) should first contact the **SPNI Field School** ① *T08-6532016, www.boker.org.il*, for advice.

Background

Kibbutz Sde Boker was founded on the fourth anniversary of the Declaration of the State of Israel, 15 May 1952. The original intention of the settlers, predominantly ex-soldiers, was to ranch cattle; hence the name Sde Boker, roughly translated from the Hebrew as 'Rancher's/Cowboy's/Farmer's Field'. Livestock rearing now plays a less important role in the agricultural economy of the kibbutz, with sophisticated irrigation techniques now producing out-of-season olives and fruits for export, as well as some cereals.

Places in Sde Boker

Ben-Gurion's Desert Home ① *T08-6560469, www.bgh.org.il, Sun-Thu 0830-1600, Fri 0830-1400, Sat 0900-1500, adults 12NIS, student/child 9NIS; guided tours by prior appointment.*
Near the entrance is a **Visitors' Centre** ① *Sun-Thu 1000-1600, Fri 1000-1400, Sat 1000-1500, adults 10NIS, child 8NIS*, where you can see a short film telling the story of the kibbutz, before walking through landscaped trees to the house. Ben-Gurion's initial stay at Sde Boker was limited to just 14 months, after which time he was drawn back into politics. He finally retired to Sde Boker with his wife Paula in 1963, living here until his death (in Tel Aviv) 10 years later. His Desert Home attracts a constant stream of Israelis to pay homage to the 'Old Man'. A well-presented exhibition illuminates his life and relationship to the Negev through letters, photos and quotes. Following this you enter the low, green prefab home, with its red roof and narrow veranda, left exactly as it was when David and Paula lived here – from the photograph of Gandhi on the bedroom wall to the packet of band-aids on the bedside table. Although now fashionably retro, it is a humble home, unlike the large stone villa built for the couple (where their graves now stand) and which he rejected as being too grand.

Ben-Gurion University of the Negev ① *Signposted 3 km south of Ben-Gurion's Desert Home is Midrashet Sde Boker, variously referred to as Ben-Gurion College of the Negev, Sde Boker Institute of Arid Zone Research, Ben Gurion University of the Negev, etc.*

Whatever title you use to refer to it, the academic speciality of this establishment is clear: the study of land and life in arid and semi-arid environments. The various institutes affiliated here attract specialists from around the world, in addition to producing much home-grown talent in this field.

Ben-Gurion Memorial National Park (Ben-Gurion's grave) The road towards the main university campus also leads to the site of David and Paula Ben-Gurion's graves. And what a place to be buried! Two simple white slabs stand amidst a landscaped park, featuring both rock and flora indigenous to the area, on the edge of a sheer rockface that provides a magnificent vista down into the canyon of the 'Wilderness of Zin'.

Ein Avdat National Park ① *T08-6555684. Daily 0800-1600; winter 0800-1500; however, arrive no later than 1300 to start a trek, as access is restricted later in the day for safety reasons. Adults 27NIS, student 21NIS, child 14NIS. Admission to both the Upper and Lower entrances is permitted on one ticket, on the same day only. The Lower 'entrance pavilion' is located by the gate to Midrashet Sde Boker, here you can buy the Sde Boker Desert Map (55NIS).*

The Nahal Zin Nature Trail provides a delightful walk along the bed of the Nahal (River) Zin, with the option of a gentle jaunt for the less intrepid (taking one to two hours), or a more strenuous one-way route (two to three hours), featuring a stiff climb up the rock-cut steps in the cliff face. There are some excellent picnic sites, as well as some peaceful spots beside that rarest of desert commodities, water pools.

Some advanced thought is required before commencing either of the routes. Both begin at the Lower Parking Lot (actually to the north, near to Sde Boker), with the long route finishing at the Upper Parking Lot (actually to the south) and the short route finishing where it began. After completing the long, one-way route, you cannot retrace your steps back to the Lower Parking Lot since it is forbidden to descend the rock-cut steps back to the valley bottom. You'll have to arrange for somebody to drive down Route 40 to the Upper Parking Lot to pick you up, or flag down a passing bus (60/392) or hitch a ride (walking back to Sde Boker along Route 40 is an unrewarding 7.5-km slog).

A good leaflet/map, describing the walk and sights on the way, is provided at the National Park entrance. **Note** Ein Avdat is a deservedly popular day-out, and thus is often crowded, with school groups during the week and everyone else on weekends and public holidays. Do not confuse the Ein Avdat National Park with the Nabatean-Roman-Byzantine city within Avdat National Park, some 11 km further south along Route 40 (see page 60).

Hiking around Sde Boker Other treks that are recommended (first get information from the Field School) include the Nahal HaVarim trek, which is best enjoyed at full moon when the white chalky paths glow and light the way. You are guaranteed to see lots of ibex. The blue trail starts from Route 14, where a brown sign points east to 'Bor HaVarim'. It's a two- to three-hour walk that finishes up near Ein Avdat. Another excellent day-trek goes from Sde Boker to Avdat (Ovdat) Nabatean ruins, taking in the Akev springs on the way. As the trail is 14 km and takes from six to eight hours, it is imperative to start as early as possible as the heat really kicks in around midday. The springs have water all year round; the upper Akev spring is a small reed-filled pool (still pleasant for a dip) while the lower Ein Akev is 20 m deep and icy.

Horvat Haluqim ⓘ *This site is to the north of Route 204, just northeast of Halukim Jct (see 'Be'er Sheva to Mizpe Ramon' map, page 34). You can walk here from Kibbutz Sde Boker.* During the United Monarchy (1004-928 BCE), a network of citadels was built in the central Negev region, each protecting state-initiated agricultural settlements. (Similarities between this process and that of the Zionist pioneers of the early 20th century are hard to ignore). Horvat Haluqim is thought to be one such 10th-century BCE fortified settlement (the original desert kibbutz?).

Today, it is still possible to see the remains of the oval-shaped fortress, with its central courtyard and seven casement rooms, plus the remains of 25 or so private dwellings that formed the agricultural settlement. The initial settlement was probably destroyed during the pharaoh Shishak's invasion in 923 BCE, though evidence suggests that the site was reoccupied in the second-third centuries CE.

Sde Boker listings

For hotel and restaurant price codes and other relevant information, see pages 12-16.

Where to stay

$$ Krivine's Guesthouse, T052-2712304, www.krivines.com. Four attractive rooms with a sense of privacy, nicely decorated, welcoming beds and a real homely feel (down to the wonky pictures on the wall and spy novels on the bookshelves). Sociable tasty meals around a huge table in the designer 'tent', garden at back (stream is planned), guests' kitchen. British John and his French wife Marion have created a warm and relaxed place that is a real pleasure to stay in. No weekend price rise. Pick up from bus stop, will drop off at Ein Avdat. Highly recommended.

$$ To the Desert, T054-7245673. On the edge of the village in the new residential development, Aviva and her husband have self-built a colourful home where 2 guest rooms enjoy plenty of space (enough for families), kitchenette, breakfast 30NIS per person, TV, roof terrace, quirky garden. No weekend price rise.

$$ Wilderness, 08-6535087/050-8671921. A spacious ground-floor apartment with quality modern furnishings, stone tiles throughout, fully equipped kitchen, feels like having your own pad. Good for families. 1 double room and sofa bed in open plan sitting room, shady garden with seating.

Kelly can provide breakfast. Discounts on stays over 1 night, price rise at weekends.
$$-$ SPNI Field School and Hamburg House, T08-6532016, www.boker.org.il, orders.boker@gmail.com. Youth hostel with roomy 6-bed dorms or double rooms, a/c with private bath, very clean, kosher dining hall (meals 38-47NIS), reservations essential (at least 2 months in advance for weekends/ hols). Adjacent Hamburg House has a further 20 a/c rooms with added comforts (TV, fridge, tea/coffee). There are great views from most of the rooms in both places, breakfast included. Prices go up Fri nights.

Restaurants

In the Midrashet's main plaza there is a well-stocked **supermarket** (Sun-Thu 0800-1900, Fri 0800-1400). The **Mitbar pub** is in the campus area, open Tue and Fri nights 2000-2400.
$$ Kha'dera, main plaza, T08-6532118. Open Sun-Thu 0900-2100, Fri 0900-1400 (take-away only). Locals were delighted when the 'Pot' opened its doors in 2010, thus doubling the choice for dining out in Sde Boker. Meals have a North African slant, all home-made, the menu changes daily (eg fried chicken, meatballs in sauce), BBQ, vegetarian option, 8 kinds of salad. Look for the little coffee wagon outside (great iced coffee and quality cakes).
$$-$ Zin Restaurant, main plaza. Open Sun-Thu 0800-2100, Fri 0800-1400. A basic

canteen-style place serving up cheap meat/veg meals (23-38NIS) and beer (12NIS).

What to do
Cycling
Geofun, Commercial Centre, Midrashet Sde Boker, T08-6553350/050-6276623, www.geofun.co.il. Mountain bike rental or guided cycling tours for all levels of experience, some suitable for very young children, some at night. Rental bikes are 80NIS per day, or 60NIS for 2 hrs plus 15NIS every extra hr during week (65NIS at weekend), map provided. Also sells bikes and accessories, and has a repair centre (the only one between Be'er Sheva and Eilat). The Sde Boker topographical map showing all trails is available here (55NIS), and the centre provides excellent information and advice – whether or not you are a customer. See website for details of week-long tours and seasonal programmes, plus they can build a full 'package' including accommodation, food, transport, etc. Open Sun-Thu 0900-1800, Fri 0830-1400, will open Sat for appointments.

Swimming
The swimming pool in the Midrashet is open Jun-Sep.

Tours
Adam Sela, organizes jeep tours around Sde Boker and Makhtesh Ramon, recommended, especially for native English speakers. **Haim**, T054-5343797. Night safaris in an 8-seater jeep (everyone gets a window), using antennae and flashlights to track animals. Haim's speciality is predators, though you may not be lucky enough to spot one of the hyenas he has managed to 'collar'. For a full jeep 640NIS for 2-2½ hrs, cheaper if fewer numbers. Also takes scorpion walks. Tea/coffee break and lots of interesting chat.

Avdat (Oboda)

ⓘ *T08-6551511, www.parks.org.il. Daily 0800-1700 (winter -1600, closes 1 hr earlier on Fri and hol eves), last entrance 1 hr before closing. Adults 27NIS, students 21NIS, child 14NIS. Combined ticket with Ein Avdat 43NIS. There is an Aroma café near the site entrance, and a Visitors' Centre, souvenir shop and toilets.*

Declared a UNESCO World Heritage Site in 2005, Avdat, (referred to by the Nabateans as Oboda) is probably the best preserved of the Nabatean remains in the Negev. As one of the major way stations on the Petra–Gaza Spice Road, Oboda also evolved as the centre of a major agricultural region. The town flourished during the Late Roman period, with the prosperity continuing into the Byzantine period. There are impressive buildings from all three periods of the town's history. The remains of the town have been substantially restored, with a line marking reconstructed areas; anything below the line indicates original remains, whilst anything above the line was reconstructed from ruins found at the site. In October 2009, however, vandals daubed paint over the churches, smashed artefacts and toppled columns, causing much damage that had not been repaired by the time of our visit. ('Avdat' is the Hebrew version of the Arabic name for Oboda, 'Abdah').

Arriving in Avdat (Oboda)
Getting there and away Avdat National Park is located on the main Be'er Sheva–Eilat road (Route 40). Be'er Sheva–Eilat Egged bus 392 sets down at the park entrance, as does the slower Metropoline bus 60 that runs every one or two hours between Be'er Sheva and Mizpe Ramon. For orientation see the 'Be'er Sheva to Mizpe Ramon' map, page 34.

Turning the desert green: how the Nabateans beat the Israelis by 2000 years

The idea that the Israelis "turned the desert green" has its origins not in the astounding contribution towards the world's knowledge of arid and semi-arid ecosystem management that Israeli scientists have made, but in a political sentiment. The implication is that prior to the return of the early Zionists, the land was 'abandoned', 'uncared for', and 'empty': thus the idea that the Palestinians had any deep attachment to the land can be negated.

However, political arguments aside, Israeli researchers have been amongst the quickest to provide evidence that they were not the first to "make the desert bloom". The Nabateans, a race probably of Arab origin, established sustainable desert agriculture in the Negev 2000 years before the foundation of the State of Israel. Their success was down to the development of sophisticated irrigation techniques.

In areas where rainfall is limited, the key factor in desert agriculture is the control of surface run-off. The loess soil of the Negev quickly develops an impermeable crust when exposed to water, thus preventing penetration into the soil of the surplus rain. By efficiently managing the control of the surface run-off, the Nabateans were able to create a system whereby each field received the water equivalent of twenty times the actual level of rainfall that falls.

Low walls dividing the water catchment area into manageable sizes also acted as conduits for directing the water. Small heaps of stones served a similar purpose, and were particularly successful in increasing the rate of water collection from light rains. Underground cisterns in adjacent farm dwellings were connected to the conduits, and allowed the prolonged storage of water. The cultivated area at the centre of the shallow wadi was terraced and walled, with the different levels of stepped terracing allowing the passage of surplus water to the field below. Along with trade on the Spice Road, the management of the water environment allowed the Nabateans to establish relatively high density settlements in this harsh desert environment.

Background

Early and Middle Nabatean period Oboda was founded as a caravan stop on the Petra–Gaza Spice Road at the end of the fourth century/beginning of the third century BCE, though the original settlement may have comprised temporary structures only, possibly tents.

The oldest Nabatean structures date to the Middle Nabatean period, in particular the reign of the Nabatean kings Obodas III (c. 28-9 BCE) and **Aretas IV** (c. 9 BCE-40 CE). In addition to becoming a centre of pottery manufacture during this period, agriculture developed significantly. The mainstay of the local economy was still the caravan route, though the rearing of goats, sheep and camels was important. The Nabatean camel corps, used to police the Spice Road, was stationed locally. The Middle Nabatean period town came to an end during the reign of the Nabatean king **Malichus II** (40-70 CE), when Oboda was destroyed by non-Nabatean Arabian tribesmen.

Late Nabatean/Late Roman period Oboda was revived in the Late Nabatean period by Rabbel II (70-106 CE), who initiated renewed agricultural activity in the region. Even the annexation of the Nabatean's empire by Rome in 106 CE failed to interrupt Oboda's expansion; indeed, it may have given it renewed impetus. The temple was re-dedicated to the local Zeus and construction began on a new Roman town to the southeast of the mound. The Emperor **Diocletian** (284-305 CE) incorporated Oboda within the defensive system of the Eastern Roman Empire, building the fortress on the east side of the mound, and recruiting local people to serve in the militia. Much building took place during this period of prosperity, though much of the Roman quarter was destroyed by an earthquake early in the fourth century CE.

Byzantine period Many of the buildings seen at Oboda today date to the Byzantine period, with the continuing prosperity being based largely upon sophisticated irrigation techniques extending the cultivated area. Grape cultivation and wine production were important to the local economic and social scene. Most of the Byzantine town, dating approximately from the mid-fourth century CE to 636 CE, occupied the west slope of the mound, comprising 350-400 homes in both houses and caves. The Christian nature of the town is evident in the substantial remains of fine churches.

With the gradual decline of the Byzantine empire, Oboda was subject to increasingly regular incursions by Arab tribesmen, with the decline in security gravely affecting the town's economic base. Oboda was finally abandoned after the Arab conquest of 636 CE.

Tour of the park
The Visitors' Centre at the entrance to the park has a short film about the Incense Route and a display of artefacts from the site. Numbers (marked in bold) refer to points marked on the Avdat National Park map, page 61. Additional detail of the mound/acropolis area is shown on the plan of 'Oboda (Avdat) Acropolis', with points of detail marked by letters in bold. From the **National Park entrance** (1), the paved road leads up a steep climb to the **upper parking lot** (6). Two points of interest, the **Burial Cave (en-Nusrah) (21)** and a **Roman villa** (8), are passed on the way up.

Burial Cave (en-Nusrah) (21) This a multi-burial site with 21 double loculi, including the graves of some women. Greek inscriptions in the vaulted entrance hall are dated to the third century CE, suggesting that the original Middle Nabatean period burial cave was later reused.

Roman villa (8) To the south of the main acropolis mound lie the remains of a Roman period villa. The plan of the building is typical of the period, with the rooms located around a central courtyard. A water cistern has been cut in the centre of the courtyard. An observation point provides an excellent view of Oboda's setting and the reconstructed Nabatean farm.

Tower This well-preserved tower stands at the southwest corner of the Late Roman period quarter. An inscription above the lintel on the tower's north wall suggests that it was built in 293-294 CE. Standing three storeys high, the tower probably served as an observation point; a function that it still retains today. Though often labelled on site plans as the 'Roman tower', it may in fact be Nabatean. The skilful architect has even contrived to make the tower earthquake proof.

Late Roman period quarter The Late Roman period quarter is probably best seen from the top of the tower. The quarter was constructed as a suburb of the early town some time in the third century CE, with building work continuing until 296 CE at least. The main street ran on a north–south axis, with most of the dwellings comprising houses built around courtyards, and constructed from well-dressed stone. The fact that there is no evidence of Christian occupation of the site suggests that the quarter had been abandoned by the Byzantine period (324-638 CE). There is a strong consensus that the quarter was destroyed by the devastating earthquake of 363 CE.

Nabatean pottery workshop (11) A brief excursion away from the main path leads right (east) to the Nabatean pottery workshop. Oboda became an important centre of pottery manufacture in the Early and Middle Nabatean periods, with a reputation for high quality and delicate workmanship. There are three distinct rooms: for clay preparation, the potter's wheel and the kiln.

Khan and Nabatean military camp There are a couple of buildings to the north and northeast of the acropolis mound that were important during the Middle and Late Nabatean periods. Neither is marked on the map.

A **khan** (caravanserai), probably dating to the Late Nabatean period and in use until the mid-fourth century CE, stands to the north of the Nabatean pottery workshop. The large building, around a central courtyard, probably stood two storeys high. The halls were used for storing goods traded along the Spice Road.

About 400 m northeast of the acropolis mound is the site of the original Nabatean military camp. The compound measures 100 sq m, with a well-built stone wall reinforced by two corner towers and two central towers on each side. The camp was the home of

Avdat National Park

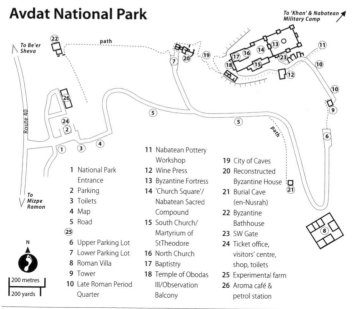

To 'Khan' & Nabatean Military Camp

To Be'er Sheva

path

To Mizpe Ramon

Route 40

N

200 metres
200 yards

1 National Park Entrance
2 Parking
3 Toilets
4 Map
5 Road
6 Upper Parking Lot
7 Lower Parking Lot
8 Roman Villa
9 Tower
10 Late Roman Period Quarter

11 Nabatean Pottery Workshop
12 Wine Press
13 Byzantine Fortress
14 'Church Square'/ Nabatean Sacred Compound
15 South Church/ Martyrium of StTheodore
16 North Church
17 Baptistry
18 Temple of Obodas III/Observation Balcony

19 City of Caves
20 Reconstructed Byzantine House
21 Burial Cave (en-Nusrah)
22 Byzantine Bathhouse
23 SW Gate
24 Ticket office, visitors' centre, shop, toilets
25 Experimental farm
26 Aroma café & petrol station

the camel corps during the Middle Nabatean period, with barracks and camel sheds still discernible. As with other Nabatean towns in the Negev, it appears that only the garrisons were housed in permanent structures, with the rest of the population almost certainly living in tents.

Byzantine fortress (13) Four wine-presses were discovered at Oboda; the best example (**12**), dating to the Byzantine period, is found by the **southwest gate** (**23**) of the fortress. The Byzantine fortress was probably built at the beginning of the fourth century CE, though much of its 2-m-thick walls was built by stone 'recycled' from the Nabatean military camp (see above) and dismantled houses. The fortress is approximately 61 m long (east–west) and 40 m wide (north–south), with twelve towers defending the walls. A deep **cistern** (**a**), with a capacity of 200 cu m, has been dug in the centre of the courtyard, supplied by two rainwater channels. In the northeast corner of the fortress is a **Late Byzantine period chapel** (**b**), built of locally quarried limestone previously used at the military camp.

Church Square/Nabatean sacred compound (14) To the west of the fortress is what was the Nabatean sacred compound during the Middle and Late Nabatean period. The construction of the adjacent churches during the Byzantine period has given the compound the moniker 'Church Square'. The sacred compound was probably built during the reign of Obodas III, to serve what is thought to be the Temple of Obodas III (see below). One of the main entrances to the acropolis is the **Nabatean gate** (**e**) in the north wall, though the portals of the gate's tower were both altered during the Byzantine period. The **cistern** (**c**) provided water to the Temple of Obodas III and stands near a **Late Roman period tower** (**d**).

South Church/ Martyrium of St Theodore (15) An epitaph on a tomb within the South Church, and the name of the same saint found engraved on fragments of a marble chancel screen, suggests that the church was dedicated to St Theodore. It was almost certainly built in the middle of the fifth century CE, but was destroyed by fire during the Arab invasion of 636 CE. The church is mono-basilical, with a central nave and two aisles divided by two rows of seven columns respectively. A three-dimensional model illustrates typical Byzantine church architecture. The Nabatean style of some of the capitals suggest that they were 'recycled' from the Nabatean temple.

North Church (16) The North Church is older, probably dating from some time in the mid to late fourth century. Again, it is thought that blocks from the former Nabatean temple were used in its construction. It is a basilica, with a single apse containing a pedestal for the bishop's seat. To the west of the atrium a flight of steps leads to the **baptistry** (**17**). The church was largely destroyed during the Arab invasion, and was particularly damaged by the act of vandalism in 2009.

Temple of Obodas III/observation balcony (18) The present observation balcony is thought to stand largely upon the site of a former Nabatean temple. Excavations have revealed the plan of a structure similar in detail to the plan of other Nabatean temples in Moab, with dedications to the deities of Dushara and Allat. Inscriptions mention various members of the Nabatean royal family, suggesting the tentative link with Obodas III, though this connection is not assured. Parts of the modern observation platform's previous functions have been identified as a **Nabatean gatehouse** (**f**), a **Nabatean portico** (**g**), and a **Byzantine entrance** (**h**).

City of Caves (19) From the observation balcony, stairs and a path descend through the main Byzantine town area, which comprised around 350 to 400 residencies. Given the nature of a typical house here, the area has been dubbed the City of Caves: many of the dwellings feature a cave cut into the hillside. The **reconstructed Byzantine house (20)** provides a good example. The complex comprises an enclosed court, with a hall to the north leading into two rock-cut chambers of the house-cave unit. The cave area almost certainly served as a wine-cellar cum pantry, in summer remaining beautifully cool, oblivious to the temperature outside. The entrance to the cave features some red ochre drawings of St George and St Theodore, with some Greek inscriptions.

Byzantine bathhouse (22) The Byzantine bathhouse is worth the extra walk since it is amongst the best-preserved structures from this period found anywhere in Israel. The left doorway from the courtyard leads into the *apodyterium*, or changing room. Beyond this room is the *tepidarium*, or lukewarm room.

Water was supplied to the bathhouse from a 64-m-deep well close by, with the waste water removed via a channel, parts of which can be seen to the north of the building. Though the ceiling of the hypocaust (the hollow space beneath the *tepidarium* and *caldarium* through which the hot air was circulated) has not survived, it is still possible to see the brick pillar bases that supported it. The furnace was to the south of the building, with the brick flues and clay pipes through which the hot air was circulated still in fine condition. The hot bath room, or *caldarium*, is on the west side of the building, and is built in the shape of a cross. The bathtubs were heated by channels fed from the hypocaust, whilst hot air was provided by a furnace to the west.

Mizpe Ramon (Mitzpe Ramon) → *For listings, see pages 66-69.*

Mizpe Ramon stands on the lip of arguably the Negev's greatest natural wonder, the Makhtesh Ramon (Ramon crater, see page 69). The town was only founded in 1956, primarily as a 17-man co-operative providing road services. Today the population stands at around 5500, swelled by the resettlement of Russian and Eastern European Jews. Without tourism, it's difficult to see any concrete economic base that could support the town, though Mizpe is becoming an increasingly popular choice for those seeking an alternative lifestyle to Tel Aviv. For the tourist, the town provides an excellent base from which to explore the stunning surrounding area.

Arriving in Mizpe Ramon (Mitzpe Ramon)
Getting there and away Mizpe Ramon is located on the northern edge of the Makhtesh Ramon, some 24 km south of Avdat National Park along Route 40. From Be'er Sheva, Egged bus 392, four per day, and Metropoline bus 60, one per hour. For details on getting down into the crater, see under 'Makhtesh Ramon' on page 69. The town centre is very compact, though it is a fair walk out to some sights.

Tourist information Visitors' Centre (details below). Staff can offer tips on hikes and driving in the region. The only problem is, by the time the centre opens at 0800, it's almost too hot to start a hike. If possible, try to call in before it closes (1600) the day before you plan to go.
SPNI Field School ⓘ *T08-6588615/6, Sun-Thu 0800-1600, Fri 0800-1200.* The Field School is about 4 km to the west of town. It is recommended that you call in here before taking a hike into the crater. Here you can also buy the SPNI 1:50,000 map (74NIS) before

attempting anything too adventurous. It's available (in Hebrew only), though the staff are willing to translate all important details. It is also a good idea to leave a copy of your planned itinerary, as the SPNI (with their communication links to the army) are your only hope of rescue if you get into difficulty.

Places in Mizpe Ramon (Mitzpe Ramon)

Mizpe Ramon Visitors' Centre ① *T08-6588691/8. Sat-Thu 0800-1600, Fri and hol eves closes 1 hr earlier. Adult 25NIS, or combined ticket with Bio-Ramon Centre 30NIS, students 21/30NIS, children 13/16NIS.*

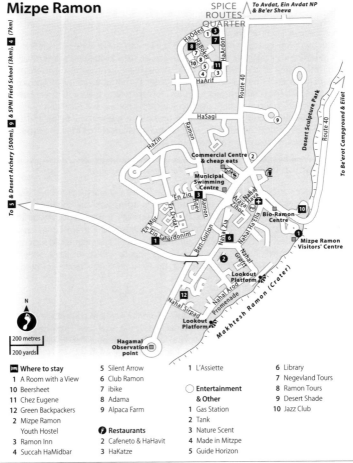

Mizpe Ramon

Where to stay		
1 A Room with a View	5 Silent Arrow	1 L'Assiette
10 Beersheet	6 Club Ramon	
11 Chez Eugene	7 ibike	○ Entertainment
12 Green Backpackers	8 Adama	& Other
2 Mizpe Ramon	9 Alpaca Farm	1 Gas Station
Youth Hostel		2 Tank
3 Ramon Inn	🍴 Restaurants	3 Nature Scent
4 Succah HaMidbar	2 Cafeneto & HaHavit	4 Made in Mitzpe
	3 HaKatze	5 Guide Horizon

6 Library	
7 Negevland Tours	
8 Ramon Tours	
9 Desert Shade	
10 Jazz Club	

A good starting point is the eye-catching Visitors' Centre, built on the crater's edge. Here you can buy a map of the Makhtesh Ramon Nature Reserve showing all the trails in the crater, and get advice from staff about hiking. The centre was being rebuilt and enhanced at the time of going to press, and promises to be an exciting introduction to the Makhtesh and its surrounding features. The cliff-top around the Visitors' Centre is often occupied by a herd of grazing ibex.

Bio-Ramon Centre ① *T08-6588755. Sat-Thu 0800-1700, Fri 0800-1600 (closes 1 hr earlier in winter). Adult 13NIS, child 7NIS, combined ticket 30/16NIS. Guided tours by prior request. Toilets.* The Bio-Ramon Centre Living Desert Museum features a tiny zoo, comprising animal, vegetable and mineral life indigenous to the crater. The collection of animal life may dissuade you from hiking in the crater: it features spiders, snakes, other reptiles, rodents and insects. Most desert creatures are nocturnal, however, and look rather wilted in their cages in the sun.

HaGamal Observation Point Staring into Makhtesh Ramon from the crater's rim is a pleasant way to pass the time, and is particularly rewarding at sundown as the rocks seemingly change colour. One of the best viewpoints is from the HaGamal Observation Point, to the southwest of the Visitors' Centre. It's so named because it is shaped like a camel.

Desert Sculpture Park To the north of the Visitors' Centre is the Desert Sculpture Park; an unusual collection of stone 'sculptures' inspired by the surrounding environment, and gathered here under the direction of the Israeli artist Ezra Orion.

Alpaca Farm ① *T08-6588047, www.alpaca.co.il. Open daily 0830-1800 (winter 0830-1630). Adult/child over 3 years 25NIS.* This unique collection of llamas and alpacas, said to be the largest herd outside South America, was gathered here some 24 years ago by an Israeli couple with a love of all things South American. The herd has grown from 180 specimens to over 600 at times, though currently it numbers around 200. A supply of high-quality wool comes out of the on-site factory – incredibly soft and non-itchy. It's possible to feed the animals, ride the llamas, and see other animals such as goats, donkeys and a camel. During Passover, there is a shearing festival (see website for details) and you can take a 'Picnicllama' for three hours (30-minute walk) into the desert with llamas loaded up with picnic hampers. The farm also has horse-riding trips to the edge of the crater, suitable for complete beginners and children (1½ hours) as well as experienced riders (two hours). Children love it here, whilst adults can enjoy some fine South American coffee in the little coffee shop. There are also four rooms available for overnight stays (see Where to stay, below).

Spice Routes Quarter The rather pretentious moniker 'Spice Routes Quarter' has not really caught on, but this is how signage refers to the old industrial part of town. Now attracting artists, entrepreneurs and those escaping the rat-race, here you can find various entertainments (see What to do, page 68), small independent shops, accommodation and plenty of practitioners of alternative medicine, acupuncture, yoga, and massage (listed on the Mizpe tourist map of the town). The disued hangars have been inventively renovated to make cool homes and offices.

Mizpe Ramon listings

For hotel and restaurant price codes and other relevant information, see pages 12-16.

Where to stay

$$$$ Beresheet Hotel, T08-6387797, www.isrotelexclusivecollection.co.uk/beresheet/. This magnificent new hotel has luxurious stone rooms (some with their own private pools) that are perched on the edge of the Makhtesh. Excellent dining options, beautiful spa and sauna, stunning outdoor pool, large indoor pool, swish bar and even a movie theatre. It really is exquisite. If you can't afford it, treat yourself to a meal or a drink in the bar with wonderful views.

$$$$ Chez Eugene, 8 HarArdon, Spice Routes Quarter, T08-6539595, www.mitzperamonhotel.co.il. Smart and contemporary hotel within an industrial loft-style space, rooms are super comfortable with fireplaces, and suites come with jacuzzi and garden. Located in the Spice Routes Quarter, the 'hip' neighbourhood in Mizpe. Be arote that access to some rooms is via the (gourmet) restaurant.

$$$$ Ramon Inn, 1 Aqev, T08-6588822, www.isrotel.com. Features studio apartments sleeping 2-6 adults (larger apartments are the best value) with kitchenette, salon, TV. Cycling packages and plenty of tour options easily arranged through the front desk. Decent sized pool but not one to relax around. No lifts – boring if you are on the 4th floor.

$$$$ Succah in the Desert, 7 km southwest of Mizpe Ramon, T6586280/052-3229496, www.succah.co.il. Recreating the desert living experience of the wandering Children of Israel during their desert Exodus, accommodation is in 'succahs': a portable dwelling made of stone walls and a palm-frond roof. Lighting and showers are solar-powered, whilst other bodily functions are performed au naturel. A central succah is used for meals, as a meeting place, meditation centre, etc. If this is your thing, it

really is superb. Reservations essential, pick up provided (it's down a rough track).

$$$ Alpaca Farm, T08-6588047, www.alpaca.co.il. Chalets overlooking the alpaca farm, 2 that suit a couple and 2 for families. Each has a shady terrace, space for campfires, roomy inside with TV, stereo, fully functioning kitchenette, a/c. Lots of light through big windows and colourful rag rugs strewn about. The isolated location means you see only stars at night. Israeli breakfast gets great reviews.

$$$ Club Ramon, T08-6586107, www.club-ramon.co.il, hotel@club-ramon.co.il. Rooms have an old-fashioned air but are bright and well-equipped with TV, fridge, kettle, a/c. Jon's Café serves beer and has reasonably priced pasta, sandwiches, etc. Breakfast included, central location. An unremarkable choice.

$$$ Room with a View, 6 Ein Sahardonim, T08-6587274. Clean, white, fresh room with, yes, a killer view from the bed, the window seat or the little garden (with loungers). Very homely and romantic, perfect for a couple. Good value and no weekend price rises; stays over 3 days get a discount. Chen's husband Yacov runs **Desert Archery**, see What to do, below. Kitchenette for self-catering. Only rules are no smoking and no cooking meat. Book in advance.

$$$-$$ ibike, 4 HaArdon, Spice Routes Quarter, T052-4367878, www.ibike.co.il. Several sparkling rooms all en suite have fluffy duvets and on-the-mark modern decor. Intimate hospitality and spirit of joining-in makes it good for lone travellers: lots of books and games in the welcoming public areas (rugs, artwork, sofas), backyard with decking, campfire, communal meals all vegetarian (soups, lasagne, all home-made and excellent quality), free tea/coffee and Wi-Fi. Very good value (includes breakfast); price rise at weekends. Bikers the main clientele but everyone welcome (see What to do, below).

$$-$ Adama, Spice Routes Quarter, T08-6595190, www.adama.org.il. Certainly a one-off (see What to do, below), this dance studio offers a variety of accommodations welcome to all. Camping outside or dorm inside the big hangar. 10 indoor plywood 'teepees' offer more privacy and come with bedding. 3 mud-brick chalets are quirky and cute and share an eccentric bathroom. Large outdoor area is delightful in a faded kind of way. Fridge, tea/coffee, no cooking facilities but healthy meals available. Very sociable, book-swap, guests can do dance classes on Sun, Mon and Tue. For 250NIS you can do a full day's dance on Sun, sleep in a tepee and get breakfast.

$$-$ Green Backpackers, 10/6 Nahal Sirpad, T054-690 7474, www.thegreen backpackers.com. The friendliest hostel in town is also completely spotless, with private rooms and cosy dorms (warm bedding). Sociable lounge, well-equipped kitchen, great advice on hikes and activities, free Wi-Fi, and the crater of Makhtesh Ramon on the doorstep. Perfect for independent travellers, and volunteers are welcomed.

$$-$ Mizpe Ramon Guest House and Youth Hostel, T08-6588443, www.iyha.org.il. Enormous place with clean single-sex 6-bed dorms which can be taken as private/family rooms (**$$**), all a/c with attached shower rooms; bedding/towels provided, TV lounges, breakfast included. Many rooms have excellent views of the crater. Internet Can get noisy at weekends.

$$-$ Silent Arrow, T052-6611561, www.hetzbasheket.com. There's no electricity in this campsite 15 mins' walk from the town centre, but there is a central campfire and a million stars. A mattress in a communal tent (sleeps 35) is 80NIS (bring a sleeping bag), or private space in one of the refurbished 'domes' is 120NIS per person. The sitting area – candlelit at night – is especially traveller-friendly, with plenty of comfy seats and a pot-bellied stove for winter evenings. Kitchen is excellently equipped (though of course there is no fridge, just cool boxes); free tea/coffee. There's space to pitch your own tent (but call in advance), mattresses provided and use of facilities (80NIS).

Recycling is practised, bathrooms clean, all-in-all a good choice. Volunteers welcome, for a minimum stay of 2 weeks (though long-term is preferred).

$$-$ SPNI Field School, T08-6588616/052-8746410. Great location west of town, right on the edge of the crater with direct access to trails, ibex grazing all around. Picnics tables, olive trees and shrubs beautify the area. Dorms often busy with school groups (50NIS). A/c doubles (week/Fri 315/415NIS incl breakfast) with attached bath, breakfast available (40NIS) and sometimes other meals if there are enough people. Essential to book in advance. Check-in 1400-2400, check-out 1100. Can pitch a tent (35NIS) but no shower unless room is vacant, so phone in advance to check; gives advice on best spots for wild camping. Good info for hikers.

$ Be'erot Campground, Makhtesh Ramon, T08-6586713. Pitch your own tent or stay in one of their Bedouin tents at this official campsite some 18 km inside the crater. Toilets (no showers), limited snack-bar, bookings and payment to be made at the Visitors' Centre. Day visitors can use the facilities for 10NIS.

Restaurants

Tel Avivian immigrants bemoan the lack of restaurants in Mizpe, but a couple of lovely places have recently opened. There is a **Supersol** supermarket (Sun-Thu 0730-2100, Fri 0700-1500) plus several falafel, shwarma and pizza places in the commercial area. The gas station is open 24/7 and has food for emergencies (it's packed on Shabbat).

$$$ Chez Eugene (see Where to stay). Daily 1900-2200. Tel Aviv style comes to Mizpe at this trendy restaurant in a converted hangar. Mediterranean fusion food, a tempting wine list, appreciative customers and a special atmosphere. Recommended.

$$ HaHavit, T08-6588226. Sun-Thu 0900-2230, Fri 0900-1400. In a new central location, 'the Barrel' serves decent meals, breakfast, bagels/sandwiches, pasta, hummus, labaneh, meat meals. It's also a nice place for a beer, with a pub atmosphere.

$$ L'Assiette, next to the Visitors' Center, T08-9317488. Sometimes they close during the low season/mid-week, otherwise open 0900-1600. With stunning views of the Makhtesh through the huge windows, this contemporary-feel cafe-bar is perfect for a light meal or a daytime drink.

$$-$ Caféneto, Nahal Zia, T08-6587777. Open Sun-Thu 0800-2300, Fri 0800-1800, Sat 0900-2200. Tasty salads, hearty breakfasts (35-53NIS). For those on a budget the mini-sandwich (Israeli omelette is good), plus coffee deal for 26NIS fills you up. There's free Wi-Fi.

$$-$ HaKatze (the Edge), 2 HaArdon, Spice Routes Quarter, T08-6595273. A family restaurant serving filling home-cooked meals (eg green curry, goulash 48NIS) and soups (20NIS); there's usually a veggie option. Alcohol available. Recommended.

Entertainment

Desert Shade, T054-6277413, www.desert-nomads.com. Head down here for sunset on a Fri night. Locals gather, as do the ibex, and a glass of wine is enjoyed with a view of the crater and sculptures in the foreground. Good hummus and fish to eat inside after dark. Off Rd 40 at the entrance to Mizpe, opposite the Spice Routes Quarter.

Jazz Club, T050-5265628, recently remodelled venue in the old industrial area. Live music (jazz/blues) on Thu nights. You'll see posters around town, or call to see what's on. Definitely worth a visit if you're in town at the weekend.

Shopping

Nature Scent, 22 HaArdon, T08-6539333, www.Natures1.com. Sun-Thu 0830-1900, Fri 0830-1600. Eco-friendly, non-animal tested, using 100% natural ingredients, this little factory produces an enormous range of lotions and potions. The soaps are excellent, particularly the scrubs; good for gifts as well as treats.

Made in Mitzpe, 21 Har Boker, T08-6595111. Sun-Thu 0900-1400 and 1600-1800, Fri 0900-1500. New age-y place selling locally made crafts, some funky jewellery, pottery, etc.

What to do
Archery

Desert Archery, T08-6587274/050-5344598, www.desertarchery.co.il, located west of town next to Silent Arrow campsite (though the 2 are not connected). Yacov has been organizing desert archery for many years. It's a non-competitive, low-impact and quite spiritual activity – developing powers of concentration as well as knowledge of oneself. Same principle as golf, but using a bow and arrow; eco-friendly as it leaves the desert as you found it. Suitable for all ages, from 6 years upwards, no minimum numbers, an incredibly reasonable 40NIS for 2 hrs' personal instruction (English speaking).

Cycling

ibike, 4 HaArdon, Spice Routes Quarter, T05 , www.ibike.co.il. Menachaim and Aviva provide excellent service for bikers going it alone or guided tours. Mountain bike hire a reasonable 70NIS per day. Also run a lovely guesthouse hotel (see Where to stay, above).

Dancing

Adama, Spice Routes Quarter, T08-6595190, www.adama.org.il. You probably didn't come to the Negev to dance, but the guys here might just change that. Founded 10 years ago by 2 professional dancers, Adama now has 8 staff and an average of 40 pupils at any one time (50/50 split Israeli/foreign). There are 3 studios for movement classes and workshops, for both professionals and novices; also yoga in the mornings. Five festivals per year (during Sukkot, Pesach etc) attract campers, musicians, all-day dancers. See website for details.

Swimming

Municipal Pool, corner of Ben-Gurion and 'En Ziq (1000-1800 most days).

Tour operators

Adam Sela, based in Sde Boker, but also does jeep tours of the Makhtesh Ramon. Good for English speakers.

Elisheva and Peter Bichel, T08-6588958/ 050-2297538. Recommended for German/ Dutch speakers.

Guide Horizon, T052-3690805, www. guidehorizon.com. Desert tourism in a buggy. Stefan also does 'packages' with accommodation in a cool hangar, a good to place to kick back after a desert trip with spa, ping-pong, sauna.

Midrashet Ramon, T08-6587042, part of the College for Judaic/Land of Israel studies. Special Shabbat observant weekends.

Negevland Tours, Har Boker, Spice Routes Quarter, T08-6595555, www.negevland.com. Reliable for jeep tours and biking.

Ramon Tours, T08-6539888/052-3962715, www.ramontours.com. Organized tours, etc.

SPNI Field School, T08-6588615. Organize free family-focused tours every Sat morning, 3-5 hrs. They are in Hebrew but, should you wish to join, phone to reserve a place. Also provides information on jeep tour and guides (who is fluent in which languages). They can provide a free map of the crater showing walking routes etc, and sell the relevant SPNI map (74NIS).

Transport

Buses stop at the Gas Station on Route 40, at the Commercial Centre on Ben Gurion, or on the road outside the Youth Hostel. **Metropoline** bus 60 runs 1-2 times per hr (0600-2200) between **Mizpe Ramon** and **Be'er Sheva** (1½ hours), passing **Avdat National Park**, **Ein Avdat National Park**, and **Sde Boker**. Egged bus 392 between **Be'er Sheva** and **Eilat** (1½ hrs) passes through in both directions 4 times per day Sun-Thu and once on Fri, though there is no guarantee that there will be empty seats.

Makhtesh Ramon

The Makhtesh Ramon can justifiably compete with the coral reefs of the Red Sea, and the unique environment of the Dead Sea, for the title of Israel's most stunning natural site. Some 40 km long, 9 km wide, and in places 400 m deep, the Makhtesh Ramon is the largest erosion crater in the world. Though comparisons with the landscapes of both the Grand Canyon and the moon are somewhat clichéd, they do serve to suggest something of the grandeur and splendour of the scenery here. Though the crater's beauty can still be appreciated from the window of a coach, this is a good place to get your walking boots on. The crater is now administered by the Nature Reserves Authority, with a number of marked walking and driving routes.

Arriving in Makhtesh Ramon The main problem with hiking in the Ramon crater is that some of the trailheads are far from Mizpe Ramon. Unless you have your own transport, take a very early bus down into the crater or are comfortable with hitchhiking, you will expend a lot of energy just getting to the trailhead. One possibility is to stay overnight at the Be'erot Campground (see 'Where to stay', page 67). It is very important to make a preliminary visit to the Visitors' Centre or SPNI Field School in Mizpe Ramon before commencing any hikes. The SPNI 1:50,000 map is invaluable (74NIS), or at the very least equip yourself with the Parks Authority map (2.5NIS).

Geology The Hebrew word *makhtesh*, meaning mortar (as in mortar and pestle), has now entered the glossary of geological terminology since it describes a geological process that has been identified only here, in the Negev. During the Miocene geological epoch,

(70 million years BP), pressure on the Earth's surface created a range of low mountains running broadly northeast-southwest through the Central Negev region. At some point the 'dome' cracked, allowing water to penetrate. Over a prolonged period the penetrating water eroded the lower, softer sandstone beneath the higher, harder limestone and dolomite, eventually creating three major erosion craters: Ramon, HaGadol and HaKatan. The term *makhtesh* is now used to describe an erosion valley surrounded by steep cliff walls and drained by a single wadi (water-course).

The layered rock beds of the cliff walls, and the bed of the makhtesh floor, display magma solidified into igneous intrusions, basalt, essexite, trachyte, clay, sandstone, mudstone, quartzite, thin layered limestone, bituminous limestone, limestone, chalk, conglomerate, flint, chert, dolomite, gypsum, ferriferous sandstone, sandstone and siltstone. What this list means to the non-geologically minded, is that the crater is full of colourful and bizarre rock formations that should not be missed.

Flora and fauna It is estimated that there are 1200 different kinds of desert vegetation in the Makhtesh Ramon, including such flowers as sun roses, hairy storkbills, Negev tulips and asphodelines. Some floral features, such as the Atlantic Terebinth (*Pistacia atlantica*), are remnants of a wetter period and provide symbols of environmental change.

The range of fauna at home in the crater is equally remarkable. You are most likely to see the crater's ibex and gazelle population, as well as raptors and other birds of prey such as Egyptian vultures, short-toed eagle, griffin vulture, kestrel and a variety of owls. Less conspicuous residents are wolves, foxes, porcupines, hyenas, and a lovely selection of snakes, spiders, scorpions and rodents. You may also come across evidence of man's occupation, dating back to Byzantine, Roman, Nabatean, Israelite and Canaanite times.

Places and hikes in Makhtesh Ramon

The importance of getting maps and checking climatic conditions at the Visitors' Centre or Field School cannot be overstressed. Enquire the day before, particularly important from October to April when flash floods are a very real threat. The 4x4 trails generally cross the crater east-west, so for walking it's best to take a north-south trajectory to avoid vehicular traffic (it's possible to hitchhike back). For those without transport and on a budget, a half-day hike leads from Mizpe into the crater, and back via the Field School (or vice versa). Starting from the promenade near the Visitors' Centre, take the green trail then the blue.

Carpenter's Workshop and Ammonite Wall The **Haminsara** or **Carpenter's Workshop** (or 'saw-mill') can be reached by driving or walking 6 km down into the Makhtesh Ramon (crater) on Route 40 from Mizpe Ramon. Alternatively, a steep walking path leads down from the cliff-top promenade to the west of the Visitors' Centre. The name is taken from the resemblance of the rock here to pieces of sawn timber. The unusual prism shapes were created by cross-fissuring under pressure in the quartzite rock. The direction of the fissures determines the number of facets (eg triangular to hexagonal). An observation platform has been built here; this poor man's Giant's Causeway takes no more than 10 minutes to view.

You can continue from here on to the **Ammonite Wall** about 5 km away. The rock face here contains hundreds of ammonite fossils, named after the ram-headed Egyptian god Ammon, whom they resemble. From here, it's a long walk back up to Mizpe Ramon, though it is possible to hitchhike or flag down a passing bus.

Short driving tour For those with their own transport, and not wishing to travel too far on foot, it is possible to make a short driving tour of some of the crater's attractions. Leaving Mizpe Ramon to the south on Route 40, the road descends the twisting 'Atzmaut Ascent' into the Ramon crater. After 6 km, a sign indicates right for the **Haminsara**, or **Carpenter's Workshop** (see above for full details).

Continuing on Route 40, take the next left at the sign for Saharonim Plateau and the **Be'erot Campground** (5.5 km away). Immediately past the campsite, the road divides. The road straight ahead leads to **Mt Ardon** (see below) after 4 km (you can drive to the base of the mountain) and to the **Ma'ale Mahmal** or 'Camel Driver's Ascent' after 10 km. This difficult ascent is one of the most dramatic sections of the Petra–Gaza Spice Road. In order to climb the face of the cliffs out of the Makhtesh Ramon, 300 m high, the Nabateans widened a natural fissure in the rock and constructed supporting terrace walls. At the top of the cliff is **Mezad Ma'ale Mahmal**, a small fort dating to the first century CE. The road is negotiable by 4WD for the first part, but the later stages are only suitable for walkers.

The right turn beyond the campsite leads to Ein Saharonim and the Saharonim Plateau. Taking the right fork, after 1.5 km the road divides again. Marked at this junction is a section of the Nabatean's Petra–Gaza Spice Road. You have to walk a little way to see anything, with the nearest preserved 'milestone' about 2 km north.

Taking the left fork first, the road leads 1 km up to the **Saharonim Plateau** to the foot of **Harut Hill**. It's possible to walk to the top of this hill, 492 m high, and back in about two hours: well worth it for the excellent views around the crater. Other options from here include following the blue markers north to **Mt Ardon** (included in the 'Mt Ardon–Ein Saharonim' hike described below), or following the black or blue markers southeast along the Wadi Ardon towards Ein Saharonim (also included in the 'Mt Ardon–Ein Saharonim' hike described below). This latter route is also passable by 4WD vehicles.

Returning to the road junction, the left fork leads a winding 2.5 km to **Ein Saharonim**. This is the site of a small spring (Ein Saharonim) and oasis, though in summer it is often dry. Also located here are the remains of a Nabatean fortress, **Mezad Sha'ar Ramon**, that served as part of the chain of stations along the Spice Road.

If you don't have a 4WD vehicle, or do not intend walking, you return the way you came. Once you have returned to Route 40, you can turn left (south), continuing for a further 2.5 km, until you see a sign on the right that indicates the **Ammonite Wall** (see above for details).

Mt Ardon–Ein Saharonim hike This is a long hike to complete in one day (seven to nine hours), and may best be split into two separate trips. The hike begins at the **Be'erot Campground**. Those on foot should note that the Be'erot Campground is 17 km from Mizpe Ramon. Bus 392 from Mizpe Ramon (heading to Eilat) will drop you at the junction on Route 40, but it's still a 5.5 km walk from here to the camp. It would be possible to hitch here but, bearing in mind the fact that you will need to make an early start, it may be best to spend the night before the trek at the Be'erot Campsite (see under Mizpe Ramon listings for details, page 67).

Turn left out of the **Be'erot Campground** and head north, ignoring the turning on your right for Ein Saharonim and Saharonim Plateau. After about 3 km, a blue marked trail leads off to the right (east), where the path begins a gradual, and then a steep ascent to the top of **Mt Ardon** (702 m). There are tremendous views from here, making the effort more than worthwhile. The descent of the south side of Mt Ardon should be undertaken with care, though once back near to the valley floor you will begin to appreciate the extraordinary coloured rock formations. This upper section of the Ardon Valley is sometimes referred to as Red Valley, due to the profusion of dark red sandstone. Dark volcanic intrusions provide some fascinating rock formations. There are also remains of fossilized trees en route. The blue trail eventually leads to Harut Hill (492 m). There are several options here: i) you can return along the unpaved road back to the Be'erot Campground (just over 3 km away; total trip four to five hours); ii) you can climb to the top of Harut Hill, and then return to the Be'erot Campground (total trip six to seven hours); iii) you can continue on to Ein Saharonim, adding a further four to five hours to what you have already completed.

Makhtesh Ramon, showing Mt Ardon-Ein Saharonim & Mt Saharonim hikes

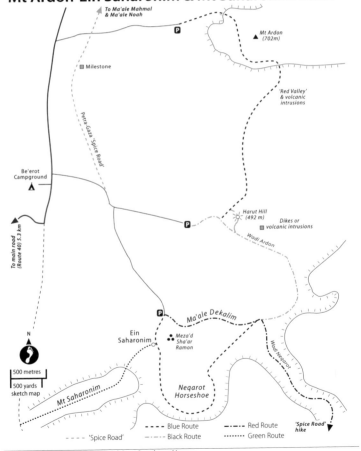

Turning left (southeast) at Harut Hill, the trail towards Ein Saharonim follows the bed of the Wadi Ardon, passing a number of spectacular volcanic rock intrusions known as **dikes**. After 2 km or so of walking, you arrive at a three-way fork. The first left red route leads southeast, into the Wadi Neqarot, and forms part of the Spice Road hike (see below). The second path is the blue route, and involves walking in the lee of some steep cliffs (with shady caves) along the **Neqarot Horseshoe** (Parsat Neqarot), and on to **Ein Saharonim**. The third route, the red trail to the right, leads west to Ein Saharonim via the **Ma'ale Dekalim** ascent. The spring at Ein Saharonim, even after a day's hard walking, is not the sort that you would wish to dive into for some relief: it's often little more than a muddy puddle. Also sited at Ein Saharonim is the Nabatean fortress of **Mezad Sha'ar Ramon**. From Ein Saharonim, it is about 3 km back to the Be'erot Campground.

Mt Saharonim hike This four- to five-hour hike also begins at the Be'erot Campground. Turn right out of the campground, and head south along the 4WD 'Oil Road'. After 4 km, a green marked trail leads left (east), ascending Mt Saharonim, on the southern edge of the Makhtesh Ramon (crater). The walk heads along the top of the cliffs, along the crater's edge, before descending to **Ein Saharonim**. On the descent to Ein Saharonim, the green trail passes **Sha'ar Ramon** (Roman Gate), where the main wadi that flows through the crater makes its exit.

Spice Road hike This is a very long trek, covering over 40 km, and best undertaken by experienced desert hikers, preferably with a local guide, and with suitable equipment for camping out. There is no reliable drinking water supply on this route. You should consult with the SPNI in Mizpe Ramon before attempting this journey, seeking the permission of their rangers, and possibly the army. You will need the SPNI 1:50,000 map. The hike emerges on to the Arava Road (see the end of the Dead Sea Region chapter).

Borot Lotz (The Loz Cisterns)

Borot Lotz refers to a series of 17 waterholes that were thought to have been first dug around the 10th century BCE, with later modifications undertaken by the Nabateans. A 4-km walking trail has been marked encompassing the best-preserved cisterns and a number of ancient remains; the whole tour takes about two hours.

Arriving in Borot Lotz (The Loz Cisterns)
Getting there and away There is no public transport to the site. To reach Borot Lotz, head north from Mizpe Ramon on Route 40, turning left (southwest) 5 km out of town at Haruhot Junction. Continue southwest on Route 171 for approximately 34 km, before turning right (northwest) on to the track at the sign for Borot Lotz. The parking lot and the beginning of the tour is 1 km along the track (taking the right fork). There are toilets, camping facilities and drinking water near the parking lot. **Note** It is forbidden to bathe in the cisterns or drink the water. Lighting fires, picking plants and flowers, and littering are all forbidden.

Background
During the reign of King Solomon (965-928 BCE), efforts were made to populate the Negev in order to provide a buffer zone between the settled kingdom and the desert nomads. Borot Lotz was part of this settlement programme along the northern ridge of the Makhtesh

Ramon. A series of cisterns were dug, primarily to store water from the winter rains, with evidence suggesting that most of the waterholes at Borot Lotz were dug during this period.

When those advanced water engineers, the Nabateans, settled in the Negev around the fourth or third century BCE, they refined the cisterns at Borot Lotz and incorporated them within their high-tech surface run-off irrigation system. Remnants of ancient farms and terraces suggest that agriculture continued at Borot Lotz until the end of the Byzantine period (seventh century CE).

Tour

Leaving the parking lot heading north, after 50 m you come to what is popularly known as the '**good water cistern**' (1), so named because of the quality of water it once supplied. The 'good water cistern' is an open cistern, cut into the soft impermeable rock and lined with a series of layers of uncut stone. Two diversion channels funnel the surface run-off water via sedimentation pools into the cistern. These pools serve to filter out silt deposits from the water.

The trail leads downhill, following an ancient drainage channel to a large cistern, 30 m in diameter, that over the years has become filled by sediment (the 'clogged cistern'). Just beyond here are the remains of a **Nabatean house** (2), probably dating to the first century CE.

Continuing downhill, in a northerly direction, lies a grove of **Atlantic Terebinth** (3) (*Pistacia atlantica*). As with other specimens of this tree elsewhere in the Negev, the presence of pistachio trees here suggests that this region was once wetter than it is now. These particular trees are thought to be several hundred years old. A diversion may be

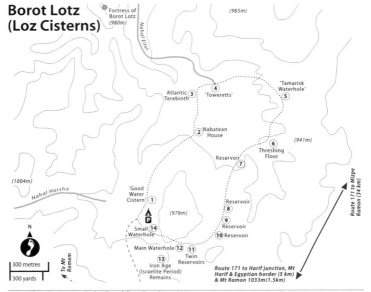

Borot Lotz
(Loz Cisterns)

Fortress of Borot Lotz (980m)

Nahal Eilot

(985m)

'Tamarisk Waterhole' (5)

Atlantic Terebinth (3) 'Toweretts' (4)

Nabatean House (2)

(941m)

Threshing Floor (6)

Reservoir (7)

(1004m)

Nahal Horsha

'Good Water Cistern' (1)

(978m)

Reservoir (8)

Reservoir (9)

Reservoir (10)

Small Waterhole (14) P

Main Waterhole (12) Twin Reservoirs (11)

Iron Age (Israelite Period) Remains (13)

N

300 metres
300 yards

To Mt Romem

Route 171 to Harif junction, Mt Harif & Egyptian border (5 km) & Mt Ramon 1033m(1.5km)

Route 171 to Mizpe Ramon (34 km)

made northwest of here to climb to the viewpoint at the top of the 980-m peak known locally as the 'Fortress of Borot Lotz'.

The trail climbs slightly to the east, following the course of a seasonal wadi. Lavender cotton, cat thyme, white wormwood and wild pyretrum grow here, and were all previously used for medicinal purposes. Also present in the riverbed are fossil remains of snails, **toweretts (4)**, that previously lived here 70 million years ago. (**Note** Do not touch.)

Climbing the ridge above you, the marked trail leads to a second cistern. This one is semi-enclosed, dug into a layer of hard, impermeable rock. The tamarisk tree growing here gives it the name, the '**tamarisk waterhole'** (5). There are remains nearby of a low stone wall; almost certainly part of the Nabatean system of surface run-off agriculture.

Ascending the next ridge, the trail leads to a **threshing floor** (6) that also probably dates to the Nabatean, or possibly Byzantine, period. It was also used in later years by Bedouins. The threshing floor stands amongst a number of ancient agricultural buildings, including livestock pens and grain storage rooms.

Crossing another dry wadi bed, the trail passes another **reservoir** (7), though this one is in a poor state of repair and seemingly overrun by saltbushes (*Atriplex halimus*). A number of **reservoirs (8) (9) (10)** further on are in far better condition. They are reached by ascending the ridge from the wadi bed, passing a number of remains of Middle Bronze Age I (2200-2000 BCE) settlements. Of the **twin reservoirs (11)** ahead, the northernmost is in the best condition, having been refurbished earlier this century.

The main **waterhole (12)** to the west is the largest at Borot Lotz, being fed by four different conduits. To the southwest of the main waterhole, off the red-and-white marked trail, lie the remains of settlements from the Iron Age, or Israelite period (1200-586 BCE) (13). The tour returns to its starting point, passing a **small waterhole (14)** on the way.

Eilat

Eilat is Israel's premier resort town, frequently billed as a hedonistic alternative to the 'cultural tourism' on offer elsewhere in the country. True, the all-year-round sunshine is a major attraction, and the undersea coral world is something that no visitor to Israel should miss, but there is some justification in the view that the tourist brochures are somewhat over-enthusiastic when describing Eilat's appeal. Development has been rapid, and though many of the larger hotels have been tastefully designed, many have not. It should also be noted that the beaches do not have the fine sand of the Mediterranean coastal resorts, but rather sand more akin to that found on the ubiquitous building sites.

However, having said all that, the town does have a very relaxed, easy-going feel, with more than enough activities available to satisfy most holidaymakers, and the north beach area is only slightly tacky. And with Israel being such a small country, attractions such as the Dead Sea or Jerusalem are never very far away.

Arriving in Eilat
Getting there and away If arriving on a package tour or charter flight, you will arrive at 'Uvda (Ovda) Airport, the military airport some 60 km to the north. Charter airlines usually arrange transport to and from Eilat and the airport: otherwise it's a 300NIS taxi fare or an irregular bus service (392 between Eilat and Be'er Sheva, four to five per day, one hour). Domestic flights use Eilat Airport, literally in the centre of town.

The Central Bus Station is located on HaTemarim, and is within easy walking distance of the hostels (though a little further from the main hotels area). Connections are good to the rest of the country, though on popular routes (Dead Sea, Jerusalem) it is as well to book seats two to four days in advance. See box, page 88, for details of buses to/from Jordan and Egypt (Sinai).

Embassies and consulates: For a full list of consulates and embassies in Eilat, see www.embassiesabroad.com/embassies-in/israel. **Egypt**, 68 Efroni, T08-6376882. In an unassuming villa west of Eilat centre. Visa services Sunday to Thursday 0900-1430, take your passport in the morning and collect after lunch. Visas (single or multiple) cost from 65-110NIS (depending on nationality; must be paid in NIS); one passport photo required.

Getting around Eilat is fairly compact and it's an easy walk between the centre and north beach area. For attractions to the south, bus 15 runs hourly from the Central Bus Station via Dolphin Reef, Coral Beach and the Underwater Observatory, to the Egyptian border at Taba (first bus 0800, last at 1800, restricted service Friday and Saturday).

Tourist information The **Eilat Tourist Office** ① *Bridge House, North Beach Promenade T08-6309111, eilatinfo@tourism.gov.il, Sun-Thu 0830-1700, Fri 0800-1300*, has lots of brochures in many languages, free maps, *Welcome Eilat* and *Sea and Sun* mags (which include discount vouchers for restaurants, etc). They also have a book swap that's worth browsing. There is a commercial **Information Office** ① *T08-6340404, Sun-Thu 0900-1800, Fri 0900-1300*, just in front of the bus station which hands out free maps and is quite helpful.

Background

Ancient history Though the modern town of Eilat was established less than 50 years ago, the advantages of this location – with its fresh water supply, natural anchorage, and commanding position on the trade crossroads between Egypt, Arabia and on to the Mediterranean – have been recognized since antiquity. When Moses led the wandering Children of Israel out of Sinai into the wilderness of Moab, he passed through here (*Deuteronomy 2:8*), and the port here was established some 3000 years ago to serve the copper mines at Timna (see page 95). During Solomon's reign (965-928 BCE), the port of Ezion-Geber had a firmly established ship-building industry (*I Kings 9:26*), and it is often speculated that the Queen of Sheba landed here on her way to visit Solomon in Jerusalem (*I Kings 10:1-2*). The Ptolemies, Nabateans, Romans, Crusaders and Mamluks all ruled Eilat, though few left any permanent mark.

The problem for archaeologists has been the positive identification of the sites of biblical Elath and Ezion-Geber. It is likely that any remains have long since been built over during the construction of the modern towns of Eilat and Aqaba, or been completely washed away by the flash-floods that periodically inundated the area. What this means for the visitor to Eilat is that there are no ancient sites in the town itself to divert you away from the beach.

Modern history The modern history of Eilat begins as recently as 1949, when the settlement was little more than a hostelry for camel caravans and a British Mandate police station. Recognizing the strategic and economic importance of access to the Red Sea, the Israeli army occupied a strip of land adjacent to the Gulf of Eilat during the closing stages of the 1948-1949 War of Independence. This territorial gain was confirmed in the Armistice Accords of 1949, a kibbutz was founded (Eilot, later moved a couple of kilometres inland), and in 1951 a port was opened. It was not until 1956 that the Israelis were able to establish the right of innocent passage through the Straits of Tiran into the Gulf of Aqaba, though Israeli ships were constantly harassed by her Arab neighbours, contrary to international law. Attempts by the Egyptians in 1967 to block the Straits to Israeli shipping was one of the factors that led to the Six Day War.

Eilat has developed considerably since then (permanent population around 50,000), and though the port remains Israel's major link to the Far East and the southern hemisphere, it is tourism that represents the town's major earner.

Places in Eilat → *For listings, see pages 82-89.*

Beaches

Though Eilat's beaches are considered its main attraction, unless you intend exploring the underwater world or partaking in the various watersports on offer, you may think that the hype is a little overdone. Most beaches are free, charging just for sun-lounge chairs (10-15NIS per day), though some do charge an admission fee. Women rarely go topless in Eilat.

Central Eilat

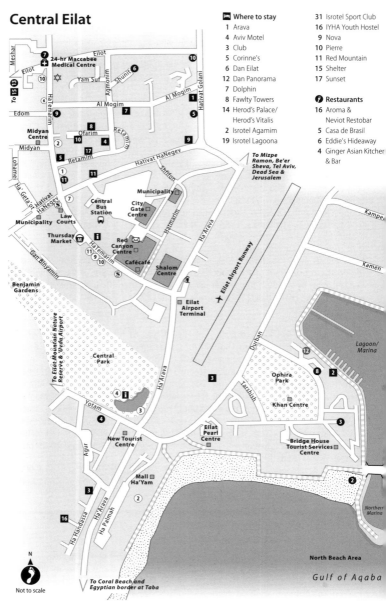

Where to stay
1 Arava
4 Aviv Motel
3 Club
5 Corinne's
6 Dan Eilat
12 Dan Panorama
7 Dolphin
8 Fawlty Towers
14 Herod's Palace/
   Herod's Vitalis
2 Isrotel Agamim
19 Isrotel Lagoona

31 Isrotel Sport Club
16 IYHA Youth Hostel
9 Nova
10 Pierre
11 Red Mountain
15 Shelter
17 Sunset

Restaurants
16 Aroma &
   Neviot Restobar
5 Casa de Brasil
6 Eddie's Hideaway
4 Ginger Asian Kitchen
   & Bar

The nearest beach to the town centre (and the most crowded) is North Beach, which is subdivided into a number of smaller beaches generally named after a nearby landmark such as a hotel (Neptune Beach, Royal Beach, etc). They have freshwater showers, bed-chairs for hire, and are generally supervised by lifeguards. A stroll along the promenade and around the lagoon/marina is a popular early evening entertainment.

Quieter beaches are to be found by heading out along the Eilat–Taba road towards the Egyptian border. Village Beach is undoubtedly one of the nicest, though it isn't large; entry and sun-beds are free. A good place for watersports is Veranda Beach, part of the Reef Hotel but if you order a drink you are left in peace. Eilat's underwater attractions are best explored at the Coral Beach Reserve (see below) and Princess Beach, where the best corals and largest variety of fish are to be seen.

Coral Beach Nature Reserve

ⓘ *Winter daily 0900-1700, summer daily 0900-1800. Adult 30NIS, student 26NIS, child 18NIS. There's a short DVD about the reef, with Dos and Don'ts.*

By far the most spectacular attraction in Eilat is the underwater world of the coral reef, populated by a diverse collection of garishly coloured fish, sharks, octopuses, crustaceans and sea-urchins. The best place to view the reef is at the Coral Beach Nature Reserve, on the Eilat–Taba road. Potential snorkellers can hire masks and snorkels here (20NIS, deposit 100NIS) and follow underwater trails through the highlights of the 1-km-long coral bed. The private beach has hot showers, sun-beds and a snack-bar. Note that 'Aqua-Sport' Beach (at the northern end) is free.

Warning There are a number of rules to bear in mind. Don't touch anything. Not only is it illegal to damage or remove anything, you may also be putting yourself at considerable risk of injury. Some of the

South of Eilat: the Eilat–Taba road

Where to stay
7 Eilat Princess
1 Isrotel Yam Suf
2 IYHA Youth Hostel
9 Le Meridien
10 Orchid
13 Orchid Reef

Restaurants
5 Last Refuge
3 Sabrest, Baruch Fish, supermarket
1 Sheikh Yousuf's Bedouin Tent
2 Village Beach Bar

Other
1 Aqua-Line Dive Centre
2 Marina Divers, Parasailing, Glass-bottom boats
4 Camel Ranch
5 Tourist Centre

creatures, whether plant or animal (or perhaps simply appearing to be a rock) are venomous, and an encounter with one of these may be an experience that you remember long after the glorious underwater colours have faded from your memory. It is recommended that you always wear some form of footwear in the water (also available for hire). If you do have an accident, even if it is just a scratch, seek immediate medical advice at the dive-shops and equipment hire places, and then consult a doctor.

Dolphin Reef

ⓘ T08-6300111, www.dolphinreef.co.il. Daily 0900-1700, pub/restaurant open later, occasional evening activities (open bar nights with good music, free entry). Beach admission adult 64NIS, student/child 44NIS. Snorkelling/diving with dolphins 280/320NIS (book in advance, includes use of beach). Relaxation pools are open from 0900-0300, over 18s only; 30/45 mins is 300/350NIS (in the actual pools, includes refreshments and use of beach).

In addition to an extremely pleasant beach with loungers, sunshades, freshwater showers and a popular pub/restaurant, Dolphin Reef also offers the opportunity to observe and swim with eight dolphins. The centre was seemingly founded for 'scientific purposes', though it is sometimes argued that this is little more than the commercial exploitation that can be found in dolphinariums the world over. However, the intentions of the centre's staff are certainly sincere and honourable. A 'supportive experience with dolphins' scheme has also proved a valuable form of therapy for emotionally disturbed children.

The admission fee entitles you to use the beach, see a natural history film and observe the dolphins from the floating observation piers. Feeding takes place a few times daily, with trainers on hand to answer questions. The other (almost secretive) activity here involves three relaxation pools (saltwater, Red Sea water, freshwater) where you can float, listening to music, at around 30 C. Numbers are limited to 20 people, and the pools are within a beautiful glorified beach hut where refreshments and further relaxing can be enjoyed, day or night.

Underwater Observatory Marine Park

ⓘ T08-6364200, www.coralworld.com/eilat. Daily 0830-1600. Park and Oceanarium adult 89NIS, child 79NIS (no student discount).Glass-bottomed boat 35/25NIS (not on Sun). Park only 79NIS/69NIS. Restaurants, souvenir shops.

If you don't want to get wet, this is the best way to see Eilat's coral world and the creatures that live within it. The Underwater Observatory comprises two large, glass-windowed rooms submerged 5 m below the sea's surface. Spectacular coral grows all around the observatory, with thousands of brightly coloured fish flitting in and out of the reef. There's a circular café within the Underwater Observatory, as well as an observation deck at the top of the tower. At over 20 m high, not only does the deck give a great view down through the clear blue sea to the coral bed below, there is also a 360° vista that takes in four countries (Israel, Egypt, Jordan, Saudi Arabia). From the pier, the **Coral 2000** glass-bottomed boat takes visitors on a 20-minute tour past the Observatory and along the reef, with explanations given in a string of languages.

Back on dry land is the **Oceanarium**, which shows a 20-minute adventure film with some 'virtual' effects (not especially exciting). There are shark, turtle and stingray pools, with set feeding times, as well as a darkened room where you can view phosphorescent fish. The Amazonians exhibition is also interesting, albeit in the wrong geographical location, plus there are rare fish aquariums and the opening of pearl oysters!

Coral Island

A popular cruise destination from Eilat is Coral Island (also known as 'Pharaoh's Island'), about 13 km south in the Gulf of Aqaba. It has been suggested that this is Solomon's port of Ezion-Geber. The lagoon on the west side of the island is not natural, and the island was used as an anchorage in later years, with fortified remains from the Hellenistic (332-37 BCE) and Byzantine periods (324-638 CE) as well as the remnants of a Crusader castle (built in 1116). The Crusader fortress was subsequently lost to Salah al-Din in 1170, recovered by Reynald of Châtillon, and lost again to the Mamluks in the 13th century.

Eilat Museum and Art Gallery

ⓘ 2, Yotam, T08-6340754, www.eilat-history.co.il. Mon-Thu 1000-2000, Fri 100-1400, Sat/hols 1200-2000, adult 10NIS, child 5NIS.

This small museum is only for people particularly fond of the development of modern Israel, although items are well displayed and there is some tourist information available. There's a short history of Eilat, from possession of the land in 1949, development of infrastructure, to present day reliance on tourism. The Art Gallery, opposite (entrance free), shows work by over 70 regional artists in ceramics, photos, paintings, jewellery, and more.

Kings City

ⓘ Eastern Lagoon, T08-6304444. Mon-Sat 1000-2000 (summer and hols 0900-2200), Sun 1000-1800. Adult 118NIS, student/child 95NIS. Free 48-hr re-entrance. Bags aren't permitted on some rides; use cloakroom outside.

This monumental 'palace' is as visually startling as Herod's hotel nearby, and it's a must if you have children. There are four sections that highlight Biblical stories (mainly about

King Solomon) in various interactive ways, plus a giant food court on the lower level. The 20-minute boat ride through the life of Solomon is rather dull until you are plunged vertically downstream, while the Journey to the Past of the pharaohs is an impressive 4D experience. The Cave of Illusions takes some time, with 70 different activities testing logical powers, games and optical illusions, plus quite terrifying dry-slides. Enquire on entry about timings of shows in English; they tend to be every two hours.

Eilat listings

For hotel and restaurant price codes and other relevant information, see pages 12-16.

🛏 Where to stay

The price categories quoted here are for the regular season, though at certain times of the year (Jewish and Christian holidays, weekends, etc) rooms must be booked well in advance (and prices sky-rocket to double or treble). Note that there are significant discounts to be had by booking through a travel agent. Eilat's budget accommodation is almost entirely confined to the area north of the Central Bus Station. **Note** This area can feel slightly seedy at night, particularly the eastern end of Al Mogim. Most of the dorm beds are 50NIS (unless it is a holiday or summer), with private doubles costing 150-200NIS (depending upon your negotiating skills). Few hostels have curfews.

Central Eilat

$$$$ Dan Eilat, North Beach, T08-6362222, www.danhotels.com. One of Israel's most luxurious hotels but still manages to retain an informal atmosphere. 8 categories of room from standard to Presidential suite, all facing the sea. **Dairy**, **Oriental**, **Brazilian** restaurants, good sports facilities and sumptuous spa, 3 beautiful pools set in landscaped gardens, off season prices surprisingly good value. Recommended.
$$$$ Herod's Palace/Herod's Vitalis, North Beach, T08-6380000, www.herodshotels.com. This place almost makes it into the 'sights' section! Herod's Palace features luxurious rooms and suites, opulent Salome Lobby built in the style of a Nabatean Temple, Four

Winds 'quiet lobby' (including romantic candlelit terrace), Officer's Club bar, Tamarind restaurant, and countless other options, Scardo shopping arcade running down to the beach, several pools, kids' pool, swim-up bar. Herod's Vitalis is a 53-room self-contained boutique spa hotel with separate check-in: over 18s only, no smoking, plus full spa facilities (not open to non-Vitalis guests). If you can afford it, stay here. If you can't, at least come and have a look. Recommended.
$$$$-$$$ Isrotel Agamim (Water Garden), North Beach, T08-6300300, www.isrotel. com. Laid-back, young hotel that aims to replicate the mellow atmosphere of a Sinai beach in the heart of Eilat. Some rooms are literally 'on the water'. Lovely pool with bar, hammocks, spa. Good choice.
$$$$-$$$ Isrotel Lagoona, King Solomon's Wharf, T08-6366666, www.isrotel.com. Isrotel-run all-inclusive hotel (all food and drink), supplement for pool views, family rooms available. Good for families, nice pool. Not a bad deal.
$$$$-$$$ Isrotel Sport Club, North Beach, T08-6303333, www.isrotel.com. Noted for its sports facilities this all-inclusive hotel has 2 outdoor pools (1 heated), kids' pool, tennis, squash, raquetball, handball, baseball, gym, jacuzzi, sauna, health centre, plus nightly entertainment.
$$$ Club, HaArava, T08-6361666, www.clubhotels.co.il. Enormous place (7 pools!), white and blue nautical exterior feeds into the interior. Rooms face pool or sea, studios for couples or suites sleeping up to 6. Don't expect service with a smile (staff are too busy), but it's a good location and lively for families.

$$$ Dan Panorama, Lagoon, T08-6389999, www.danhotels.com. Fairly large rooms with marina views (no sea views), balconies, plus some suites with jacuzzi on balcony. Considerable price hike at weekends and holidays. Looks rather dated but has all the amenities you require.

$$$ Nova Like, Hativat HaNegev, T08-6382444, www.atlashotels.co.il. Large Atlas hotel set around a decent-sized pool. Good for children, not for those after peace and quiet. Energetic vibe. Rooms are large enough and brightly furnished. Worth paying extra for a balcony.

$$$ Pierre, 123 Ofarim Alley, T08-6326601/2, www.scuba.co.il. Double and triple a/c rooms with freshly painted white walls and new linens, flatscreen TVs. Shared balconies on each floor and a couple of good seating areas – particularly the breezy 5th-floor terrace. Good discounts with Marina Divers, or hotel-diving packages can be arranged. Price includes continental breakfast, free internet/wireless. Well managed, friendly, recommended.

$$$-$$ Aviv Motel, 128 Ofarim Alley, T08-6374660, www.avivhostel.co.il. Bright light rooms, many with big balcony (some sea views) or cheaper without; a/c, TV, fridge, kettle, sink, plates. Small pool with dusty loungers. Continental breakfast included. Very good value.

$$ Fawlty Towers Motel, 116/1 Ofarim Alley, T08-6325578. Some of the cheapest doubles around, at 150NIS, singles 120NIS, simple and clean, a/c, attached bath. Definitely demand an upstairs room with tiny balcony not downstairs which feels dingy. Wi-Fi access, no breakfast or kitchen.

$$ Dolphin, 99/1 Almogim, T08-6326650/050-7904594. Don't get too excited about the pool/jacuzzi (it's the size of a bathtub) but 6-bed dorms are large, mainly with single (rather than bunk) beds, and have fridge, microwave, TV. A bit scruffy but cheerful. Small backyard. Double room 150NIS.

$$ Red Mountain, 137 Hativat HaNegev, T08-6363222, redmountain@012.net.il.

Reasonable value for typical hotel room, though smells slightly fusty. Central location, a/c, TV, OK pool.

$$ Sunset Motel, 130/1 Retamim, T08-6373817, www.sunsetmotel.co.il. Good-value decent double rooms with fridge, TV, attached bath, around a small but quiet back garden. Single rooms less appealing as they're tiny and open out on to rather noisy bar area, but for 100NIS not bad. 2 buildings: the one on the north side of the street has superior rooms though they are same price.

$$-$ Arava, 106 HaAlmogim, T08-6374687, www.a55.co.il. Clean popular dorms and fairly priced private rooms (doubles 160-180NIS depending on season) with a/c, fridge, TVs; singles and triples also available. Luggage storage (10NIS per day), laundry service, cheap snorkelling equipment rental, 2 kitchens, charge for tea/coffee, breakfast available, free Wi-Fi or internet 12NIS per hr. Owner, Aron (T052-3445027) also has a couple of large apartments for rent which are excellent value, sleeping 2-6 people, with garden, kitchen, TV.

$$-$ Corinne, 127/1 Retamim, T08-6371472, www.corinnehostel.com. Reasonable a/c mixed-sex 8-bed dorms with attached bath (though a little dark, as in the basement) attract long-stayers. Plenty of storage space, free sheets, fridge. Cosy a/c wooden cabins (180NIS) weirdly have reindeer cut-outs galloping across the roof, attached bath, TV, clean and quiet. No breakfast but little kitchen is adequately equipped. Jolly management.

$$-$ IYHA Guest House and Youth Hostel, HaArava, T02-5945605, www.iyha.org.il. Clean single-sex a/c dorms with TV, fridge, kettle (100NIS), or private singles/doubles/triples (245/320/495NIS), reservations recommended, price hike in high season and at weekends. Clean and well run. Couple of nice seating areas on balconies looking out to sea. Free Wi-Fi.

$$-$ The Shelter, 149/1 Eshel, T08-6332868, www.shelterhostel.com, pex@actcom.co.il. Run by Jews who believe that Jesus was the Messiah, this villa converted into an appealing guesthouse is split into male and female halves. Rooms/dorms are small and cheap (150/50NIS), free sheets, towels, tea and coffee, no breakfast but use of kitchen, delightful succah set up in the garden with comfy sofas as well as plenty of space to chill outside. Unmarried couples can't share rooms, curfew 2400, Bible studies at 1100, no drugs/alcohol/smoking permitted.

South of Eilat

Shady camping is available at the (**$**) SPNI **Field School** at Coral Beach, with good amenities to hand. Camping on the beach is legal away from the town centre, though is perhaps unsafe for lone women, and a noisy road runs right next to the beach.

$$$$ Eilat Princess, Eilat–Taba Rd, T08-6365555, www.eilatprincess.com. One of Eilat's best hotels. Real sense of luxury, all rooms with extra large beds, some beautiful suites and themed 'club' rooms (Indian, Thai, Moroccan, Russian, etc), 3 restaurants, good bar and club, series of swimming pools connected by waterfalls and slides, gym and health centre, tennis, private beach. Good choice if you can afford it. Recommended.

$$$$ Isrotel Yam Suf, Coral Beach, T08-6382222, www.isrotel.co.il. Busy, comfortable hotel with the Red Sea Sports Club and Manta Diving Centre on site, great pools and plenty of sun-loungers, kids' club, happy families everywhere, decent restaurants and well located.

$$$$ Orchid, Coral Beach, Eilat–Taba Rd, T08-6360360, www.orchidhotel.co.il. Beautiful Thai-style resort village featuring a variety of chalets, older wooden ones among little gardens, larger (newer) Shangri La chalets moving up the hillside, peaking in an incredible villa with private pool. All have sea-facing balconies and are tastefully furnished with immense beds. Picturesque pool area, lovely loungers, private beach (a walk away), bike rental, free shuttle to city, supervised kids' entertainment. A good choice, but staff rather off-hand.

$$$ Orchid Reef, Eilat–Taba Rd, T08-6364444, www.reefhoteleilat.com. Beachside location is excellent, spacious rooms all have balconies with sea views, decent pool. Recently refurbished with modern decor and facilities. Not bad value (unless it's Israeli holidays). Reasonably priced spa. Junior suites and suites also available.

$$-$ SPNI Field School, Coral Beach, Eilat–Taba Rd, T6371127, www.teva.org.il. Private a/c rooms, breakfast included, sleep up to 8 people; prices go up Jul-Aug and hols. Camping in pleasant shady picnic area with clean shower blocks (breakfast 40NIS), convenient for beach.

❶ Restaurants

Central Eilat

Most of the falafel/shwarma stands and bakeries are located along HaTemarim. The nearest big supermarket to the hostels area is at the junction of HaTemarim and Eilot; there is also a Supersol at the back of the Red Canyon Mall.

$$$ K2, T08-6337222. Daily 1200-2400. Gets the prize for Eilat's funkiest lighting. 5 types of Asian food. Highly recommended. Impressively chic, but do diners really want a TV at their table?

$$$ Ranch House, Royal Beach Promenade, T08-6368989. Open 1900-2300, except Fri. Expensive American steak house using beef imported from the US. Wang's Grill next door has sophisticated interior and excellent, but expensive, Asian-American cuisine.

$$$-$$ Casa Do Brasil, T08-6323032. Daily 1200-2400. Good music and professional staff. Popular Brazilian grill restaurant has a mellow outdoor terrace filled with plants and a themed indoor area. Carnivores come for a meat feast, the all-you-can-eat deal involves 11 kinds of meat including lamb, chicken, veal, chorizo, liver and heart. The pizza/pasta is a tamer option (58NIS) or salmon steaks (89NIS) and burgers (78NIS) are generous.

$$$-$$ Eddie's Hide-A-Way, 68 Almogim (off Eilot), T08-6371137. Open Mon-Thu

1800-2300, Fri 1730-2330, Sat 1400-2330. Perennial favourite since 1979, best known for its steaks and fish dishes. Reservations recommended. Decor is unfussy: smart white table cloths and simple wooden furniture.

$$$-$$ Ginger Asian Kitchen and Bar, T08-6372517, www.gingereilat.com. Daily 1200-2400. Excellent, busy restaurant mixing Asian cuisines: Japanese rice dishes and sushi, Thai noodles and fish mains, Malay and Indonesian noodles, good soups. Prices from 18-108NIS. Interior of clean lines and black furniture. Popular for takeaways.

$$$-$$ La Cuccina, Royal Beach Promenade, T08-6368932. Daily 1830-2300. Very good Italian food and not grossly overpriced considering the location: pizzas, steaks, fish, interesting pastas. Make sure to book a seat in the elegant outdoor area as the interior is rather 80s by comparison.

$$$-$$ Santa Fe, T08-6338081, www. santa-fe.co.il. Fusing Israeli favourites with vaguely Mexican-influenced cuisine, this restaurant has become a popular place of late. Comfortable interior, pretty laid back, decent background tunes.

$$$-$$ Little Brazil, 3 Eilot, T08-6372018. Sun-Fri 1800-2300, Sat 1300-2300. "Meet: A lot of Meat", says it all really, though they do actually recognize vegetarianism. All-you-can-eat meat deals: adults 146NIS, children (up to 12 years) 55NIS, veggies 65NIS, fish 98NIS, stews and salads, mains 62-90NIS. Cosy front room preferable to larger rear restaurant.

$$ Gulf Restaurant, T08-6374545. Open 1200-late. A busy old-school restaurant lit by fairy lights. Pleasant terrace. Wide menu that is not overpriced (good special offers), kosher grilled meat and fish, lots of kebabs, steaks and skewers; for vegetarians it's pasta, pizza, salads.

$$ Il Pentolino, 112 HaTemarim, T08-5343430, www.ilpentilino.com. Sun-Thu 0800-2400, Fri 0800-1500, Sat end of Shabbat-2400. Huge choice of (kosher) pasta, bagels, salads, pizza etc. Always busy with a mix of customers. Relaxed terrace, warm and casual indoor area, candlelit in the evening but also a good spot for breakfast. Does take-away.

$$-$ Shibolim, Eilot, T08-6323932. Sun-Thu 0700-2130, Fri 0700-1400. Dairy kosher restaurant that is attractively rustic in decor and menu, with wide choice of borekas (22NIS), salads, sandwiches, excellent breakfasts (30-35NIS). Recommended.

$$-$ HaLev HaRahav, HaTemarim, T08-6371919. 'The Wide Heart' serves excellent Middle Eastern food, felafel, kebab, schwarma. Extremely popular – look for the tables outside packed with locals day and night.

$ Pizza Lek, 134 HaTemarim, T08-6341330. Open 1100-0230. Perfect for that emergency pizza slice, green olive particularly delicious, kosher, takeaway or eat in.

South of Eilat

$$$ Sabrest, Coral Beach, T08-6379830. Daily 1230-2230. Seafood with Middle Eastern and almost French twists, plus Israeli grill, fish (89-102NIS), aged steaks (102-159NIS), seafood stew. Lovely large terrace or contemporary ambiance inside, padded orange leather sofas mixed with Asian design. Intimately laid out with partitions between some tables, makes the most of an essentially bland square space.

$$$ The Last Refuge, Coral Beach, T08-6373627, www.hamiflat.co.il. Daily 1230-2300. Considered by Israelis (local and holidaymakers) to be the best seafood restaurant in town. Main dishes 60-90NIS, plenty of choice on the menu. Appealingly decked out with nautical equipment, fishing nets on the ceiling and gingham tablecloths.

$$$-$$ Baruch Fish Restaurant, Coral Beach, T052-2769749. Sun-Thu 1200-1530 and1800-2400, Fri and Sat 1200-2400. Catch of the day – ask for advice – and requests (such as roasted veg accompaniments or salad) are catered for. A cosier place than most, small and narrow and with a personal touch.

$$-$ Aroma, next to Isrotel Yam Suf, Coral Beach. Daily 0730-2300. Reliable old Aroma for good salads, sandwiches, drinks; a/c.

🎵 Bars and clubs

There is a density of pubs around the Tourist Centre, all much of a muchness (backpacker/budget orientated, they get going late). Swankier options are along the promenade of North Beach or those along the Eilat–Taba road (particularly Coral Beach area) which are chiefly beach bars. For nargila and snacks head to Sheikh Yousuf's **Bedouin Tent**, near Coral Beach, a good places to be at sunset. Open till midnight.

Neviot Restobar, North Beach, T08-6379989. Open till 2400 or later. Attractive central bar area, decking, cane furniture, shaded by sheets of sails, 1+1 deals from 1900-2100, serves breakfast 0900-1400. Nice atmosphere.

Taverna, Tourist Centre. Open 24 hrs. 'The first and oldest pub in Eilat.' Backpackers' bar. Beer and meals reasonably cheap. Rather raucous. Live music.

The Three Monkeys, Royal Beach Promenade. Daily 0830-0230. 'Plastic' English pub (makes a change from 'plastic' Irish pubs), nevertheless one of the most popular. Live music; shows football games.

Underground, Tourist Centre. Open 24 hrs. Popular with backpackers. Cheap beer and food, loud music and hard drinking, sports shown on giant screen.

Unplugged, Tourist Centre, T08-6326299. Cosy sofas, very busy in the evening, beer cheap, good value meals, shows movies or plays loud music; pool table is a feature. Quite nice.

Village Beach Bar, Coral Beach, T08-6375410. Sun-Thu 0830-2100, Fri/Sat 0830-0400 Great little beach with palm shades and mellow music, where you can hit the beers (16-20NIS) from your sun-lounger. Also decent (if limited) food menu.

The top hotels have fairly unatmospheric nightclubs. A more enjoyable time is likely at the various beach parties that are usually held near Coral Beach (ask around in hostels). Nothing gets going in Eilat much before midnight. 'Club nights' come and go at places in the Industrial Area; ask young locals or hostel staff what's 'in'.

🎭 Entertainment

Casinos

You will have to cross the border to Egypt for gambling, to the **Hilton Taba** casino, www.tabapoker.com, passport required. There has been talk of a casino opening in Eilat, but it is yet to happen.

Cinemas

Red Canyon, Red Canyon Centre, HaTemarim. The triangular landmark of IMAX-3D unfortunately has screenings chiefly in Hebrew with only the occasional English film. Tickets are 79NIS which includes a stroll through the mini wax museum.

🎉 Festivals

For further details and precise dates contact the **Tourist Information Office** (T08-6309111, eilatinfo@tourism.gov.il). **Red Sea Classical Music Festival**: an international festival held late Dec/early Jan. **Chamber Music Festival** each Feb. **Jazz on the Red Sea**: extremely popular 4-day jazz festival, last week in Aug. **Teymaniyada**: 3-day celebration of the Middle East (music, singing, dancing, food) in Aug.

🛍 Shopping

Books

Steimatzky have branches on the Promenade and in Mall Ha'Yam.

Market

There's a market every Thu on Hatmarim, opposite the bus station.

Shopping centres

Mall Ha'Yam, North Shore, eclipses Eilat's older malls and is conveniently located. Significantly cheaper, however, is the BIG Shopping Centre in the industrial area north of the city centre, a 20 NIS taxi ride away. There are plenty of designer shops along the Promenade of North Beach.

⚙ What to do

Birdwatching
Eilat is on the main migration route between Africa and Europe, via the Great Syrian-African Rift Valley, with about 430 species of migratory birds having been observed in the region. 40 different species of raptors alone have been noted here. The main birdwatching area is the **Bird Sanctuary**, a disused rubbish tip turned into a nature park with indigenous flora. Guided tours and various birding trips are available, contact the International **Birding and Research Centre**, T08-6335339, eilatbirding-blogspot.co.uk. International birdwatching week runs from mid-Mar.

Cycling
Holit Desert Tours, office at Khan Centre (opposite Dan Panorama), T08-6318318, www.israelpetratours.com. Guided tours (for families also), or quality bikes for rent, maps provided.

Diving
There are numerous companies offering diving and dive equipment rental. Note that you have to pay for mandatory insurance. Experienced divers must have had at least 1 dive in the last 6 months, otherwise will have to do a refresher dive (around 200NIS). Most dive centres offer SSI or PADI certification. Yosefal Hospital has a decompression chamber. Most of the dive companies also hire out snorkelling gear for 30-40NIS per day, though hiring from a hostel is cheaper (eg Arava Hostel has equipment for 15NIS per day). The prices below are the going rate at the time of writing: full equipment rental (including unlimited air refill) 150NIS; introductory dive 220-240NIS; private guided dive 160-180NIS, 2 dives 200NIS, 3 dives 290NIS,

including equipment; guided night dive 300NIS; boat dive to Japanese Gardens 170NIS; boat trip to Coral Island (including 2 dives, full equipment, lunch) 390NIS; dive with dolphins 225-300NIS; SSI Open Water 5-day course €295 (1500NIS) not including student record (maximum €80 extra); 2 Star Advanced 2-day course 600NIS.

The following operators are long-established and provide English instruction (with plenty of advance warning): **Aqua Sport**, Coral Beach, T08-6334404, www.aqua-sport.com; **Coral Sea Divers**, Coral Beach, T08-6370337, www.coralsea.co.il; **Isrotel Manta Diving Club**, Yam Suf Hotel, T08-6382240, www.redseasports.co.il; **Lucky Divers**, 5 Tzukim, T08-6335990, www.luckydivers.com; **Marina Divers**, near Reef Hotel, Eilat–Taba Rd, T08-6376787, www.scuba.co.il. **Snuba**, South Beach, T08-6372722, www.snuba.co.il. 'Snuba' is similar to diving except that the tank remains on a small raft on the surface (ages 8 and above, max depth 6 m, approx 1 hr, 180NIS). Good location by the Caves Reef which is rich in marine life.

Glass-bottom boat tours
Coral 2000, Underwater Observatory, T08-6373214, Israel-Yam, T08-6332325, www.israel-yam.co.il. Daily cruises at 1030, 1130 and 1530 for 2 hrs to the Jordan and Egypt borders via Coral Reserve and Japanese Gardens. Bar; upper deck for sunbathing.

Hiking
SPNI Field School, Coral Beach, Eilat–Taba Rd, T08-6326468, office on the 1st floor, Sun-Thu 0800-1800. The best source for information on hiking in the region. They also sell the 1:50,000 map of the Eilat Mountain Reserve (the only sheet that has been translated into English).

Horse and camel riding
Camel Ranch, Wadi Shlomo, T08-6370022, www.camelranch.co.il. Morning and late afternoon excursions along the wadi, or you

Excursions into Sinai and Jordan from Eilat

Many visitors to Eilat (particularly those on package tours) like to book short trips across Israel's borders into Jordan and Sinai (Egypt). A one-day trip to Petra in Jordan (allowing you around four hours at Petra) will cost around US$160-180 excluding visas (available on the border, US$14) and border taxes (about US$20 total). Four hours is nowhere near enough time at Petra (one-two full days is really the minimum to fully appreciate it), but if this is your only chance to visit then you must go for it. A two-day tour to Petra and Wadi Rhum will cost around US$400-450, including accommodation and food but excluding visas/border taxes.

A one-day trip to St Catherine's Monastery at the foot of Mount Sinai costs around US$135 (a 'Sinai permit' is available on the border) plus border taxes (under US$30 total). For those wanting to book a tour to Egypt (and not just Sinai), they will require a full tourist visa (not available on the border but easily available at the Egyptian Consulate in Eilat).

If you are good at planning in advance, booking a trip before you get to Eilat could be cheaper. You can book a one-day tour through **Fun Time**, based in Jerusalem, 24-hour T054-4904105, www.fun-time.org.il.

can try 'Solomon's Chariots' (a chariot being a donkey-cart ride).

Watersports
There are numerous companies in Eilat offering a variety of watersports. The following prices are about the going rates. Boating: canoe 60NIS per hr; motorboat 200NIS per hr; speed boat 650NIS per hr. Parasailing: 140NIS per 10 mins. Waterskiing: 120NIS per 10 mins; 200NIS per 20-min lesson.

Tour operators
Kite X Club, Veranda Beach, T08-6373123, www.kitexeilat.co.il. Courses and equipment for potential and experienced kite-surfers.
Paradise Tours, T08-6323300, www.reservation.co.il. Daily tours to Petra, St Catherine's (everything included except border tax and tips), Masada/Dead Sea (US$150), Jerusalem (US$150), and all Eilat's activities (fair prices).
Thru Us Travel, T08-6316886. www.thru ustravel.com. Range of options including 1-day tours to Petra (US$139 excluding visa fees and border taxes, service described as

'impeccable' by one reader), 2-day tours to Cairo (US$170), cheaper if booked online.
Yacht Venus, T050-8444770, www.yacht venus.com. Tours to Coral Island and Taba, with drinks and BBQ.

⊖ Transport

Air
Airline offices Arkia, Red Canyon Mall, T08-6384888, www.arkia. IsrAir, www.israir airlines.com, Shalom Centre, T08-6340666.

Air'Uvda (Ovda) Airport, T08-6375880, T03-9723302, is located some 60 km north of Eilat (1 hr along Route 12), and handles most international flights. Since it is primarily a military airport it is not shown on some maps. Bus 392 passes the airport 5 times per day (only twice on Fri), or a taxi between the airport and Eilat will cost around 300NIS. If arriving on a package tour, transfers are usually arranged for you. There is a tourist information counter, cafeteria and a bank.

Eilat Airport, T08-6373553, T03-9723302, is slap bang in the city centre (the travel brochures don't mention the noise when they describe Eilat), and handles mainly domestic flights run by **Arkia**, **IsrAir** and **El Al**. You can probably walk there from most hotels (otherwise it's a short taxi ride or bus 15 stops outside).

Bus
The Central Bus Station is on HaTemarim (information T08-6368111, 2800*). During holidays and high season tickets should be reserved at least 2 days in advance. There is an information office and phone information service. There are toilets, left luggage and snack places.

Be'er Sheva via **Mitzpe Ramon** (Route 12): Bus 392, Sun-Thu 5 per day 0630-1700, Fri/Sat 2 per day, 3 hrs. **Haifa** (via Be'er Sheva, Hadera and Netanya): Bus 991, Sun-Thu 0900, 2400, Fri 0900, Sat 1530 and 2400, 6 hrs. **Jerusalem** via **'En Boqeq**, **Masada** (2 hrs 20 mins), **Ein Gedi** (3 hrs): Bus 444, Sun-Thu 0700 1000 1415 1700, Fri 0700 1000 1300, Sat 1630 and 2130 (peak season), 5 hrs. **Tel Aviv** via Arava: Bus 393

and 394, Sun-Thu 11 per day from 0500-0100, Fri 5 per day 0500-1500, Sat 11 per day 1130-0100.

For details on getting to **Jordan** and **Sinai** (Egypt), see box, page 88, and Getting there, page 8.

Car hire
The following firms are all found in the Shalom Centre: **Avis**, T08-6373164, www.avis.co.il. **Budget**, T08-6374124, www.budget.co.il. **Eldan**, T08-6374027, www.eldan.co.il. **Sixt**, T08-6373511, www.sixt.co.il.

Taxis
Drivers must always use their meters, although in Eilat they often refuse. Fares are the same whatever the number of passengers (maximum 4). There's an extra charge 2100-0500. They can charge 2NIS per piece of luggage (and are entitled to charge 2NIS extra for telephone call-outs). **King Solomon's**, T08-6332424. **Taba**, T08-6333339.

Hikes around Eilat

The area above Eilat has been declared the Eilat Mountain Nature Reserve, and provides some excellent hiking ground. The reserve extends as far north as Timna Park, bounded on the west by the Egypt/Israel border, and on the east by the Edom Mountains in Jordan. With the three major rock types found here being dark hard igneous, red stained sandstone, and lighter yellow sandstone, the area is marked by some stunning rock formations in bright, vivid colours.

Hiking information
The only drawback to hiking here is that few of the trailheads can be reached by regular public transport. None of the routes described below has drinking water en route, so you must bring your own (minimum 2-3 litres per person). It is not recommended that you walk during the middle of the day, so an early start is necessary, and summer is certainly not a good time to undertake these hikes. Sun-block and a sun-hat are essential. It is a good idea to tell someone exactly where you are going, and what time you are due back. **Note** The hiking maps below are for general information only, and should not be seen as a substitute for the SPNI 1:50,000 hiking map of the area around Eilat. This is the only sheet of the series that has been translated into English, and it is strongly recommended that you buy it if you intend making any of these hikes.

Mt Tz'Fahot hike

This hike offers good views of the Gulf of Aqaba, with the advantage that it is accessible by public transport. The trail is fairly easy, taking two to three hours. To reach the trailhead, take bus 15 from Eilat to the turn-off for Wadi Shlomo camel ranch (see map, page 80).

The trail begins at the estuary of the Shlomo River, at the turning for the camel ranch. The path leads upstream for some 2 km, where it meets the Wadi Tz'Fahot (1). Continue along the path of the Wadi Tz'Fahot, with its numerous acacia trees in its bed, in a southerly direction. The valley becomes narrower, and is joined by a small waterfall to the right (west) (2). About 250 m beyond here the path forks (3). A black-marked path leads right (west) towards the Gishron River, though we take the left, green trail. The path starts to climb up the ravine quite steeply (4), before a narrow valley joins from the right (south) (5). It's a tough slog up this last stretch, until you eventually reach the top of 278-m Mt Tz'Fahot (6). The views down to the Gulf of Aqaba are particularly attractive in the late afternoon light, though the temptation to wait around for the sunset must be avoided, since this will require a difficult descent in the dark. The trail is marked down the east side of the mountain, joining the Garinit River, and reaching the beach area at the Coral Beach Nature Reserve. Bus 15 runs back to Eilat from here.

Mt Tz'Fahot hike

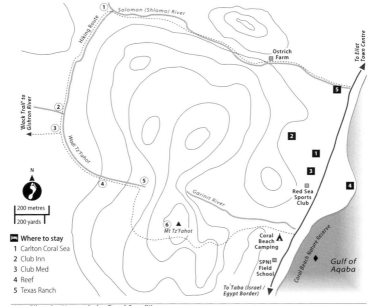

Where to stay
1 Carlton Coral Sea
2 Club Inn
3 Club Med
4 Reef
5 Texas Ranch

Mt Shlomo hike

This is quite a long hike (five to six hours), beginning from Route 12 to the northwest of Eilat, and finishing on Route 90 (Arava Road) to the north of Eilat. Unless you want an uninspiring walk back into town, you'll have to arrange for someone to pick you up from where the hike finishes. The hike features an excellent view from the top of Mt Shlomo, as well as passing numerous waterfalls of varying size. The trailhead is reached by leaving Eilat to the west, on Route 12. After 7 km, a sign indicates right for Mt Shlomo (Solomon's Mountain). Irregular bus 392 from Eilat runs along Route 12 (see Transport, page 89).

Leaving the parking lot (1), head north along the course of the Solomon River. The cleave through which the river runs was formed as a result of the process that created the Great Syrian-African Rift Valley. Continue north along the riverbed until you come to a point where two stream beds join the Solomon River (2). Follow the course of the stream to the east (right) until you reach the mountain's saddle (3). A path leads up to the observation point at the top of Mt Shlomo (4), from where there are terrific views of the surrounding area. Particularly impressive is the view into Moon Valley, in the Sinai to the west.

Descend Mt Shlomo on the path to the east, dropping down to the bed of the Mapalim River (5). The walk north along the riverbed is most attractive, passing a number of waterfalls. The height and power of the water will depend upon the season (they may be dry in summer), though it's usually possible to walk through them all. You eventually reach a point where there are two falls together (6). Turn right (east) here, and follow the trail until you reach the Netafim River (7). After walking for a half-hour or so, you reach a point that is accessible by vehicle from Route 90 (8). If you are not being picked up here, it is a 4-km walk down to Eilat.

Mt Shlomo Hike

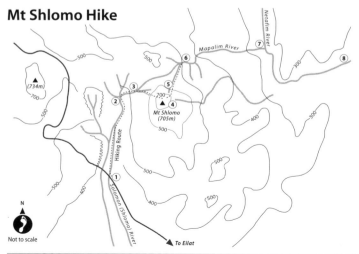

Ein Netafim and Mt Yoash hike

This short hike is in two parts. The first section visits Ein Netafim, a perennial spring above Eilat, where there is a good chance of seeing some bird and animal life. The second section of the hike visits the Mt Yoash Observation Point, from where there are excellent views of the surrounding area, with the option of continuing down to the Gishron River. Total walking time is around 2½ hours for the two early sections, five to six hours if you continue on to the Gishron River hike. The trailhead is reached by leaving Eilat to the west on Route 12. After 10.5 km, a sign on the left indicates Mt Yoash whilst a sign on the right points towards Ein Netafim. Bus 392 from Eilat runs along Route 12.

Turning right off Route 12, there is a sort of parking lot (**1**). It is possible to drive further down towards Ein Netafim and park there, but you will almost certainly be reluctant to take a hire car down here. It's a 20-minute walk down the twisting dirt path and across a dry wadi, to the lower parking lot (**2**). Having arrived at the head of the waterfall (dry), it is a treacherous descent to the spring below. You often see mountain goats here, who apparently assemble to have a good laugh at the humans attempting the narrow paths.

Having reached the bottom of the waterfall, hopefully in one piece, take the path marked in black along the right bank of the Netafim River (**3**). The path is marked by green powdered shards that, when wet, form a clayey substance from which pottery is made. After several minutes walking, a series of rock-cut steps lead down to a section of superbly coloured sandstone, with a collection of hues from pale yellow, through deep reds, to purple. Crossing the riverbed, you turn left, after several minutes reaching the head of the spring (**4**). It is not uncommon to see wildlife assembled around the spring. In addition to the goats, rabbits and rodents, quite a lot of birdlife congregates here, including the Desert Swallow and the Onychognathus Tristami, with its orange-tipped wings. Though Ein Netafim is a perennial spring, this does not mean that the flow of water will be much more than a trickle flowing into a muddy puddle during the hotter months of the year. The pool here is not natural, having been built by the British in 1942, and later refurbished.

From here, you can either retrace your steps, or follow the green trail signs back up to the lower parking lot (**2**).

To do the second section of the hike, return to the upper parking lot (**1**), and drive diagonally across Route 12 to the turning marked 'Mt Yoash'. About 100 m along this

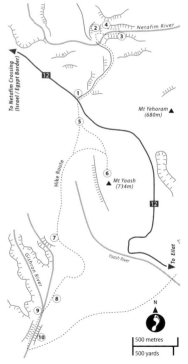

Ein Netafim & Mt Yoash hike

trail is a parking lot (**5**), from where it is a 20-minute walk along the path on the left to the top of the 734-m Mt Yoash (**6**). (You can take a 4WD vehicle all the way up here). The observation point here has great views over the whole Gulf of Aqaba, with Jordan and Saudi Arabia clearly visible across the water. The Sinai Desert, in Egypt, is to the west, whilst the dark mountain to the north is Mt Shlomo (Solomon). On the return to the parking lot, it is possible to make a left turn and walk down to the Gishron River Observation Point (**7**).

From here, you can follow the blue trail markings down to the Upper Gishron River, or return to your car. If you descend to the river, about 1 km further along the river course is a 20-m-high waterfall (**8**). You can climb around the falls on a path to the right just before it. The path continues along the right bank of the river, passing a number of rock drawings illustrating ships, camels, goats and a mounted rider (**9**). Follow the green trail into the narrow crevice to the left (**10**). This pass is reputedly named after a larger than average girl, Tsafra, who was unable to squeeze through! The narrow canyon reaches the Yehoshafat River, then passes through the saddle between the Yehoshafat and Solomon Rivers, before reaching Route 12 several kilometres south of the turning for Mt Yoash.

Mt Hizqiyyahu Observation Point and Moon Valley

This is not really a hike, but the observation point here is worth visiting for the fine views it offers, particularly of Moon Valley. The observation point is 300 m east of Route 12, at a point 18 km from Eilat (and 6 km from the Netafim crossing point into Egypt). Irregular bus 392 from Eilat runs along Route 12. Information boards at the two viewpoints here explain the topography of the land. The view into the moonscape of Moon Valley, across the border in Sinai, is amazing. It is also possible to see the Egyptian military guard post across the border, as well as the UN base that was used to monitor the international border.

Red Canyon hike

This is one of the best short hikes in the Eilat Mountain Nature Reserve and is suitable for all ages, though there are a couple of steep descents using ladders, and one steep ascent. Total walking time is two to 2½ hours. The trailhead is reached by leaving Eilat to the west, on Route 12, to the junction for the Netafim border crossing point into Egypt after 11.5 km. Irregular bus 392 from Eilat runs along Route 12 (see page 89). The road bears right (northeast) here, and after a further 10 km a sign indicates right for Red Canyon. Take this unpaved road (but reasonably good, even for a hire car), taking the right fork after 1 km (the left fork, indicated as Old Petra Road emerges back on to Route 12 about 11 km further on).

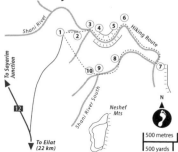

Red Canyon hike

After 1.5 km, you reach the parking spot (**1**).

Follow the path leading from the parking lot. After five minutes walking, there is the option of dropping down into the ravine on your left, or continuing along the path above it. The upper path eventually drops down into the ravine (**2**). There are some stunningly coloured rocks here, including some very vivid purples. Turning right, after several minutes walking, the ravine is joined from the left by the course of the Shani River (**3**). This is a seasonal wadi, dry for most of the year, though its bed is the habitat of a number of plants adapted to the seasonal drought and extreme temperatures. These include the Raetam bush, identifiable by its stork-like branches, which are bare for most of the year but sprout small green leaves and then flower after the rains. (It is forbidden to touch or pick any plants).

As you continue along the ravine, another small wadi joins from the right. The ravine begins to narrow significantly, until you reach the Red Canyon (**4**). The Red Canyon was created by the cutting action of the Shani River. Ferrous acids give the rock its deep red colour, with higher concentrations of acid producing the darker reds. Water and wind action created the beautiful shapes in the canyon. Where the canyon narrows, there are a series of metal hand rails to help you down. (**Note** After a couple of hours in the sun, the metal rails can become red-hot to touch.) The canyon subsequently becomes even narrower, with some metal steps placed to help your descent. Further metal steps drop down another level, where the canyon walls provide some deliciously cool and welcome shade.

The narrow canyon emerges into a wider one, where a sign (**5**) offers you the option of climbing back above the Red Canyon and returning to the parking lot (about one hour), or continuing on the green route along the Shani River. The latter is recommended. The Shani River takes a sharp southeast turn (**6**), marked by a green clay wall to the left. The riverbed is dotted with numerous Tamarisk trees that not only sink deep roots into the ground, but have also evolved a system whereby salt is excreted onto their leaves, collecting the night dew and then feeding off the dew as it drops to the ground. The salt left on the ground around the tree deters competitors for the water nearby.

After a further 500 m, the Shani River is joined by another ravine from the right (west) (**7**). Turn right into this narrow ravine, and follow its gently uphill sloping course (marked by black trail signs). Numerous rock rabbits (*Procavia capanis*) can be seen scuttling about here. After several hundred metres, the black trail markers indicate an ascent to the left, above the dry waterfall (**8**). The path here is very steep and care must be taken. Follow the black trail markers past the large acacia tree (**9**) until a junction is reached (**10**). The black route bears left, following the course of the Shani River South towards the dark bulk of the Neshef Mountains, before reaching the main road (Route 12) near to the turn-off for Red Canyon. The better route, however, is to turn right at the junction (**10**) and follow the red trail markers back to the parking area. This last section is quite up and down, and frustrating in that you keep thinking that the parking lot will be just over the next rise. It's easy to feel disorientated, but keep to the main path and it will lead to the parking lot.

Amran's Pillars hike

This hike begins from Route 90, about 12 km north of Eilat, where a sign (with blue-and-white and green-and-white trail markers) indicates the hiking routes. Going north, you cannot turn left at this point but have to continue on to Be'er Ora Jct. From there, you can backtrack to the south and the turn-off for Amran's Pillars. The track leads 5.5 km to Amran's Pillars (though it is signposted as '6.5 km').

The track is unpaved, though with care you should be able to get a car along. After 2.5 km the path forks (with the route to the left following the green-and-white trail along the Nahal Shehoret for the Black Canyon hike) and the right fork following the blue-and-white trail to Amran's Pillars. After about 2.5 km, the rock formations become stunning, with the lines of faulted and folded strata displayed at the surface in beautiful blacks, reds, browns and greens. Less than 500 m further on you reach Amran's Pillars. Yellow buttressed cliffs top the huge eroded red columns of sandstone that form the pillars. They may not be as large or domineering as Solomon's Pillars in Timna National Park, but the colouration of the rock here is certainly more strident.

Arava

From the Gulf of Aqaba to the Dead Sea is a strip of desert known as the Arava, the largest region in Israel but home to just 3000 people. The Arava Road (Route 90) follows the course of the great Syrian-African Rift Valley, an extension of the East African Rift Valley (see box, page 97). Here exist isolated yet vibrant kibbutzim, each with a distinct atmosphere and outlook, which are interesting places to stop for a night or two. Hiking is good in several areas, while the pink Edom mountains of Jordan against the hazy desert plains make for some spectacular vistas.

Timna Park

ⓘ *T08-6316756, www.timna-park.co.il. Sat-Thu 0800-1600, Fri and hols 0800-1500. Last entry is at 1600 but the exit gates are not locked so you can leave any time. Adult 44NIS, student/child 39NIS, separate entry for Tabernacle 15NIS (last tour at 1530), night tours 69/59NIS (Jul, Aug and hols). Tickets valid for 3 days. An A4 map (showing touring trails) is provided, however, the Easy Guide booklet (10NIS, 15NIS with CD) lists 16 walking trails, has much clearer maps and is strongly recommended. A 15-min multi-media video about the park is shown at the entrance. Ask about timings in English.*

Timna Park covers 60 sq km and is an expanse of unusual rock formations, stunning views, archaeological sites, and the oldest known copper mines in the world. The contrasting colours of pink canyons, cream cliffs, black mountains and white-sand wadi beds give Timna a powerful beauty. A variety of hiking and driving trails are marked through the park, taking in the most spectacular and unusual sights, and requiring different levels of physical exertion, from seven hours walking to no more than 30 minutes away from the car.

Arriving in Timna Park
Getting there and away Timna Park is 27 km north of Eilat on Route 90, Egged buses 393 and 444 from Eilat (20 minutes, 15NIS) can drop you at the turning to the site (from where it's 3 km to the entrance). **Note** Get off by the brown sign for Timna Park, and not the first blue sign for Timna Mines. Returning to Eilat requires standing by the main road and flagging down any passing vehicles. Most Eilat travel agents run tours to Timna Park.

Getting around The driving tour can also be undertaken on foot, though hikers should be aware that most of the attractions are 3-4 km apart. It is possible to hitch rides between sites if you don't have a car. Bikes can be rented at the lake, where you can also buy a map of trails or check (and photograph) the map board displayed at the start of the trails. If you intend undertaking any walking routes, you must be suitably equipped with a plentiful water supply, sun-block and a wide-brimmed hat. It is advisable that you inform the park staff at the entrance where you intend going, how long you plan to take, and to check in with them when you complete your trip. The staff will also give you a map and advice on the walking trails. Keep to the marked paths, and beware of unmarked (and very deep) mine shafts.

Geology

The park is encircled on three sides by the high Timna Cliffs, formed of light-coloured geologically continental sandstone, overlaid with marine sedimentary rock stacked in distinct layers of dolomite, limestone and marl. Copper carbonate ore nodules, mixed with azurite, cuprite and paratacamite, as well as copper silicate deposits, are located at the base of the cliffs and provided the basis of the substantial copper mining and smelting industry that developed here. The Timna Cliffs are open on the east side, from where the four wadis of the valley (Wadi Timna, Nehustan, Mangan and Nimra) drain into the Arava depression. At the centre of the park stands the Mt Timna plateau, a darker igneous intrusion of granite and syenite.

Background

The copper mines at Timna were once popularly known as 'King Solomon's Mines', with the Bible relating how Solomon (965-928 BCE) derived great wealth from the export of this valuable commodity. However, copper mining and production at Timna predates Solomon by a considerable period and, further, there is no archaeological evidence that suggests that the people of Israel or Judah were engaged in any form of mining in this area. In fact, the Bible makes no actual reference to King Solomon's Mines, and it is probably true that throughout the period of the United Monarchy and the subsequent Kingdoms of Judah and Israel, the mines at Timna lay abandoned.

Excavations suggest that quarrying for copper ore and primitive copper-smelting began at Timna around 6000 years ago. The most intense period of activity at the site was during the 19th and 20th dynasties of the Egyptian New Kingdom (c. 1320-

Dead Sea south to Eilat: the Arava road

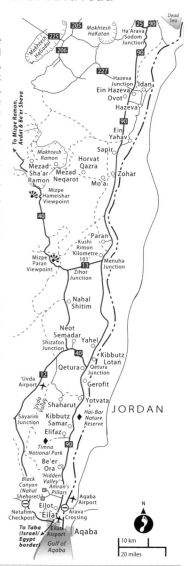

The Arava

The Arava is part of the Syrian-African Rift Valley, formed in antiquity when this whole region lay under the ocean, with only the granite peaks of Sinai protruding above sea level, and great deposits of limestone laid upon the ocean-bed. Early in the Miocene epoch, pressure on the earth's surface from both east and west caused the limestone to rise above the water in two long, north–south running folds. The violent rupture of the strata between the two folds, and the subsequent slumping of the land between the two north–south linear faults, created the Syrian-African Rift Valley.

The northern section of the Rift Valley (north of the Dead Sea) is dominated by the Jordan River. The southern section (south of the Dead Sea to the Gulf of Aqaba) is occupied by the Wadi Arava (Arabic 'Arabah); a highly braided stream that only occasionally has water. The two sections are separated by a diagonal ridge of limestone that contrived to shut in a section of the old ocean bed complete with a large quantity of salt water; hence the Dead Sea. The Jordan River and the Wadi Arava form Israel's eastern border with Jordan.

The Wadi Arava is a wide wadi in the north, with several broad lateral valleys. The western, Israeli, side of the wadi is defined by the ranges of the Tih, and the eastern side by the west-facing scarp of the Jordanian Heights. Throughout the northern Wadi Arava the indigenous vegetation is sparse, according with the highly saline and alkaline nature of the soils, especially in the area of the plains around Sodom. Further south, beginning some 50 km north of Eilat (near the mines of Timna) the valley bottom looks like a poor savannah area with a scattering of acacia and tamarisk and indigenous salt bushes and grasses surviving throughout the year.

Above the valley itself the land rises steeply to the west, with elevations immediately adjacent standing at 476 m at Yahel and elsewhere at 200-400 m, rising inland west of Yotvata to 710 m.

1085 BCE), with mining continuing through the Iron Age IA-IIB (c. 1200-700 BCE), and periodically through to the second century CE of the Roman period. Production in the region has subsequently continued from the beginning of the Early Arab period (638 CE) until present day.

Places in Timna Park

This is the main marked route, total tour time is about four hours (on foot) or an hour if you whip round in a car. Head out along the bed of the Wadi Timna, passing the Mt Timna plateau to your left. After 3.5 km, turn right at the sign for the Mushroom, Chariots and Arches. Follow the road for 5.5 km to the arches (other sights you will visit on the way back).

The arches and ancient mines From the car park, follow the blue-and-white arrow up the steps. These lead to a series of attractive rock formations in the white sandstone at the foot of the cliffs, most notably the arches created by wind and water erosion. This area was one of the major mining centres, with approximately 10,000 shafts found in the immediate vicinity. The Late Chalcolithic shaft-and-gallery system mines found here (c. 3300 BCE) are the earliest known examples of such copper mining techniques, while many of the Egyptian New Kingdom shaft-and-gallery mines (c. 1550-1000 BCE) display a level of sophistication only known previously in Roman or later period mine engineering. You can follow a red trail through the arch (using metal rungs at times) and on past the 'cave of the Egyptian miner', until the trail forks. The black trail leads to a observation point with panoramic views, via a ladder, and then rejoins the red trail. The red trail continues down the wadi, then look for the blue trail which climbs out on to a low hill. Here is a mine shaft 37 m deep (which you can enter) plus an all-round view of the area. The saucer-shapes that are visible all around are actually silt-filled mining shafts that were dug through the rock cover into the sandstone below. The route descends back towards the car park. It takes no more than one hour. Return to the road, and turn left at the sign for the Chariots (2.5 km).

The Chariots A steep, marked path leads to a cliff-face that contains a number of drawings thought to date from the Egyptian/Midianite era. The Midianites, along with the Kenites, were a northern Arabian people who operated many of the Egyptian mines in the region. The drawings on the sandstone cliffs feature deer and ostriches, plus a chariot drawn by ibexes. A walkway leads into a canyon where it is possible to see the better preserved chariot drawings. On the right are oxen-drawn chariots containing Egyptian soldiers armed with shields and axes. In the centre a group of hunters handle dagger, bows and arrows. This short walk takes around 20 minutes.

The Mushroom and the smelting camps Although the Mushroom, a perfect example of desert erosion, is the main photo opportunity, the importance of this site lies in the New Kingdom smelting camp located here (c. 13th-12th centuries BCE). Within a fenced-off area lie the remains of a number of buildings that were formerly accommodation units and storerooms around the main courtyard of the smelting camp. Four furnaces were discovered here, now in the Eretz Israel Museum in Tel Aviv. Amongst the many finds at this site was a corbeled vault containing the remains of two Proto-Boskopoid skeletons of African origin. In a fenced-off area, 70 m to the west of the smelting camp, is a sacred ceremonial place, used by miners of ancient times.

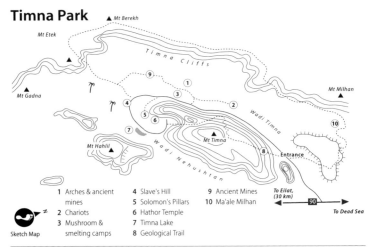

Timna Park

1 Arches & ancient mines	4 Slave's Hill	9 Ancient Mines
2 Chariots	5 Solomon's Pillars	10 Ma'ale Milhan
3 Mushroom & smelting camps	6 Hathor Temple	
	7 Timna Lake	
Sketch Map	8 Geological Trail	

Returning to the junction on the main road from the park entrance, turn right (west). Take the first left, leading to Slave's Hill, Solomon's Pillars and the Hathor Temple.

Slave's Hill Approximately 500 m along this road, to your right, is a low hill labelled Slave's Hill (though there is no explanation as to why this name has been given). This is the site of a large smelting camp dating to the 14th to 12th centuries BCE, with some evidence of a brief period of reoccupation in the 10th century BCE. The camp was surrounded by a strong defensive wall, parts of which remain, with two towers guarding the entrance gateway.

Solomon's Pillars Further along the road (1 km), you come to Timna Park's most outstanding natural phenomenon: huge eroded columns of Nubian sandstone known as Solomon's Pillars. It is thought that the 'pillars' here were created by water seeping into deep cracks that formed in the sandstone cliffs of Mt Timna during the creation of the Great Syrian-African Rift Valley. The pillars are particularly attractive in the late afternoon light (if they're not obscured by tour coaches that is). Metal steps up the rock to the right lead through an arch to some Egyptian rock carvings, though it's very difficult to make them out (look through the nearby 'telescope' to locate the hieroglyphs on the rock face). The view alone, however, is worth the climb. The path descends via steps to the Hathor Temple.

Hathor Temple The discovery of the Hathor Temple by Rothenberg in 1966 proved conclusively that the copper mining activities in the southern Negev region were controlled by the Egyptian pharaohs, in collaboration with the Midianites (though local people were employed as workers). An open shrine was built here on the site of Chalcolithic remains during the reign of the Egyptian pharaoh Seti I (1318-1304 BCE). The temple appears to have been rebuilt numerous times, having been severely damaged by earthquakes on at least one occasion. Vast quantities of votive offerings, both Egyptian and Midianite, were found within the site.

Timna Lake and Tabernacle (7) Going back to the main road, it's then 3.5 km on to Timna Lake. By foot, it's quicker to follow the gravel track past the temple and around the edge of Mt Timna (about 40-minutes' walk). The attractive man-made lake provides a welcome splash of blue in the parched, semi-arid environment. The park entry ticket includes use of the pedalos on the lake, plus plastic bottles to fill with coloured sand as a memento. Next to the lake are shaded picnic tables, a souvenir and snack shop, and the pleasant **King Solomon's Inn** which serves simple but good food until 1700, eg Middle Eastern meal for 2 (69NIS), pitta and hummus (15NIS), salad plates (18-25NIS). You can hire bikes at the lake and get a trail map from the shop (see Getting around, page 95). A five-minute walk away is the Tabernacle, a reconstruction of the 'portable dwelling place for the divine presence' that accompanied the Israelites as they wandered the desert (*Exodus 25:8-10*). Entrance is with a guide only (set times displayed outside, last entrance 1530), though you may be permitted a quick look having come all this way. It is also possible to camp at the lake (44NIS per person).

Walking Trails The trails can be used to link some of the main sites, or done just for their own sake. The Easy Guide lists 16 trails and it is strongly recommended to buy a copy if you are intending to do some trekking. Three of the best trails are listed below:

The Geological Trail begins at the park entrance, and climbs up the east side of Mt Timna for breathtaking views of the surrounding valley from the granite plateau. The trail follows red markers and Israel National Trail markers, simultaneously, while boards explain geological features on the way. It descends at Solomon's Pillars after around three hours, from where it's an hour's walk back to the park entrance.

The Arches, Ancient Mines and Canyons Trail is a three- to four-hour hike begins at the arches car park (though this is actually 7 km from the park entrance). Follow the blue signs until you come to the signpost marked 'Roman Cave, White and Pink Canyons, Solomon's Pillars'. The trail then follows black-and-white trail markers along the course of the Wadi Timna bed, via the sites known as Roman Cave, White Canyon and Pink Canyon, before arriving at Slave's Hill and Solomon's Pillars. The hike can be done just as well in reverse, and is especially attractive and scenic.

The Ma'ale Milhan, Timna Cliffs and Mt Berekh hike is the most demanding of all the trails, taking around seven hours but providing some excellent views. The hike begins at the park entrance, heading north, skirting the bases of Sasgon Hill and Mt Mikhrot. There is then a steep ascent, Ma'ale Milhan to Mt Milhan. The route passes along the top of Timna Cliffs, providing great views into the valley below, before making a descent between Mt Berekh and Mt Etek. The trail then joins up with the latter stages of the Arches, Ancient Mines and Canyons trail.

Hai-Bar Yotvata Wildlife Reserve

ⓘ *Route 90, T08-6376018, www.parks.org.il. Sun-Thu 0830-1700, Fri and Sat 0830-1600. Adults 27NIS, children 13NIS, Predator Centre additional 25/13NIS or combination ticket 43/22NIS. Call ahead to book tours. Camping 50/40NIS.*

This reserve is located off Route 90 (Arava Road) about 35 km north of Eilat. It has its origins in the Hai-Bar Society, founded in the 1960s with the twin aims of reintroducing populations of wild animals indigenous to Israel, and to protect existing endangered species. Under the administration of the Nature Reserves Authority, Hai-Bar has developed significantly, and reintroduced many animals mentioned in the Bible, such as the Arabian oryx, African wild ass and onagers. Some species not indigenous to Israel, such as addax and Scimitar-horned oryx, are being bred for reintroduction into their original habitats abroad. A successful predators breeding centre, featuring canines, felines, hyenas, raptors and reptiles, was established in 1986.

There are three sections to the reserve. The first section is the open area, where the various species are left to wander in a quasi-natural space. The Predators Centre features a number of endangered species, plus an 'unpleasant' collection of rodents and scorpions. There is also a large enclosure housing a variety of vultures. The reserve also features a Desert Night Life Exhibition Hall, where it is possible to observe nocturnal and semi-nocturnal wildlife. Feeding time is a must. To tour the reserve 'safari-style' you need a vehicle. A CD which gives information about the animals (in English) is available.

Kibbutz Lotan → *For listings, see pages 102-103.*

Getting there and away Lotan is 50 km north of Eilat, about 2 km east of Route 90. Egged buses 394/444 to/from Eilat pass by the turning to Lotan, though you will have to flag down a lift to get you to the kibbutz gate.

Formed in 1983, Lotan was founded in the collective spirit by young idealists of mixed nationalities. Unlike early kibbutzim, members are religious, although it is a Reform Judaism that is practised here with strong egalitarian values. Lotan trod an ecological path, which has branched into successful eco-tourism ventures, as well as setting a standard for the region in green living. The kibbutz is now a member of the Global Ecovillage Network. It is a pretty, peaceful and intriguing village, with low homes hidden by flowering shrubs and bikes on the pathways being the main form of transport. The Eco-khef (eco-fun) centre is a working model of organic gardening, composting and water recycling where tours and workshops take place. Other activities include hiking, watsu (see What to do, page 103) or admiring the large herd of dairy goats. A nature and bird reserve on the southern edge of the village attracts migratory species; early morning is a good time to observe the birds from hides. Near the reserve is one of Israel's last remaining sand dunes, best at sunset when the light is particularly romantic.

The seven-week Green Apprenticeship course (usually starting December), attracts overseas students to study organic gardening, ecological design, alternative building methods and permaculture. Volunteers of all ages and creeds are also welcomed, and find it an extremely satisfying episode in their lives, learning skills to carry into a greener future as well as experiencing communal life. Students and volunteers live in the Bustan (Arabic for 'garden'), a prototype for sustainable living in 'adobe igloos' built of straw, tyres and mud by the students themselves, See www.kibbutzlotan.com for details of the GA and also about the Peace, Justice and the Environment programme.

Neot Semadar

Getting there and away Neot Semadar is located just off Route 40, about 60 km due north of Eilat. Bus 382/392 passes Shizafon Junction (five to six times per day) from where someone can pick up. From Neot Semadar, the drive east down the Shayarot Cliffs towards the Arava (along Rd 40) is a spectacular one.

The kibbutz of Neot Semadar (population 160) seems to be crammed with talented craftspeople from both the artistic and culinary realms. Located 65 km north of Eilat, the community was established in 1989 by a group of friends, and now a constant stream of volunteers boosts their numbers. Fifteen years of hard work have resulted in the creation of an Arts and Crafts Centre to provide workshop space for the local artisans. The resultant building is quite a sight to behold: a fluid structure in the spirit of Gaudi, towering above a garden of roses and painted a distinctive salmon-pink colour, incorporating wrought iron, stained glass, ceramics and mosaics. The 'passive' air-conditioning tower is central to the design, plus walls nearly a metre thick also serve to keep the building cool. There are wood-workers and metal-workers, weavers, potters, silk-screen artists and more. The shop sells pieces by the different artists and it's an interesting mix of conventional and innovative design, with items that are useful as well as decorative. You need to call in advance to arrange a **guided visit** ① *T08-6358170, www.neot-semadar.com, 35NIS per* *person including visit to the winery, lasts 1-1½ hrs, no tours during Shabbat or on holidays).* The kibbutz is also famed for its high-quality organic produce (especially from the herd of dairy goats). This can be sampled in their vegetarian restaurant (see Restaurants, below), which is justifiably famous.

Arava listings

For hotel and restaurant price codes and other relevant information, see pages 12-16.

Where to stay

$$$ Kibbutz Lotan Guesthouse, T08-6356935/054-9799030, www.kibbutzlotan. com. The original kibbutz houses have been clad in mud and turned into charming guest rooms, decorated with desert colours (request one of the newly refurbished ones), fridge, sink, hot drinks, and lots of space outside to hang around. Wi-Fi, a/c, no TV. Communal meals are taken in the dining hall at set hours. Prices go up Thu-Sat and hols. Breakfast is included, meals 25-35NIS, Shabbat dinner 45NIS. Guests get a free eco-tour and use of the seasonal swimming pool (Passover-Sep). The kibbutz pub is open Wed and Fri from 2200.

$$-$ Desert Inn (Khan Aviran), Peran, T08-6581821/052-3868938, www.han-aviran. co.il. Around a central grassy garden with palm trees and a water feature, 3 rooms have en suites, a/c, TV and can fit families. A further 5 rooms have just mattresses, pillows, clean sheets, air cooler, and sleep up to 15 (sleeping bag/towel provided in emergencies). These can be taken as dorm beds (though groups aren't mixed together). Big kitchen (limited equipment), good shared bathroom facilities. Large outdoor jacuzzi under a palm shelter is attractive, space for campfires, tables and chairs. Impressive and delicious buffet breakfast taken in the farmhouse-style dining room (dinner only for groups over 10). Owners Amos and Shuli are immensely likeable. Current prices posted on website. Moshav bar is open on Fri nights and use of swimming pool is free. Turn at brown sign for Khan Avitan/Peran from Rd 90,

1 hr north of Eilat. Pick up from bus stop, or from INT trail.

Restaurants

The **grocery shop** in moshav Peran is open Sun-Thu 0800-1400 and 1730-2100, Fri 0800-1400.

$$ Café Cartouch, Kibbutz Yahel, T052-4564089. Wed and Thu 1700-2300, Fri 0900-1600, Sat 0900-1400 and 1700-late. Light meals, quiches, nice setting.

$$ Pundak Ne'ot Semadar (Inn), Shizafon Junction, Ne'ot Semadar, T08-6358180. Open Sun-Thu 0700-2100, Fri 0700-1600, Sat 1800-2100 (kitchen closes 1 hr earlier than times shown). Vegetarian organic restaurant (virtually all ingredients made on the kibbutz), breakfasts, light mains, divine frozen yoghurt, fresh juices, salads. They've managed to create a special atmosphere that is unpretentious and relaxing. The pretty interior has a wood stove for winter evenings, in daytime the sunlight filters through the leaves of many plants, no music, heavenly garden at the back. Also ideal for an evening drink – the kibbutz wine is excellent. Store sells dates, olives, wine, yogurt, etc.

$$ The Teahouse, Kibbutz Lotan, T054-9799050. Sun-Wed 1000-1600, Thu 1000-1600 and 2000-2300, Fri 1000-1300. Healthy vegetarian food, soufflés, pies, sandwiches, soups (mushroom if you're lucky); all home-made right down to the bread. As far as possible, Minna uses produce from Lotan, be it dairy or veg from the garden. Local beer available. The unusual octagonal building has windows in all walls and is nicely decorated with piles of cushions, rattan rugs and local artwork on display. There is a little shop, selling further works by artists from the community.

$$ Yotvata Inn, Yotvata, T08-6357449. Sun-Thu 24 hrs, Fri until 1700, Sat from 1000. Most people visiting Yotvata see little more than this roadhouse, made famous by its fabulous selection of dairy products produced at the kibbutz and sold throughout the country. Meat meals, snacks, sandwiches and, of course, ice cream and awesome chocolate milk.

What to do
Camel Riders, Sharahut, T08-6373218/054-4956030, www.camel-riders.com. A desert tours company based at Sharahut, 22 km south of Shizzafon Jct, ie in the middle of nowhere. Tours explore the southern tip of the Negev, from 90 mins (75NIS) to 6 days, allowing you to reach places otherwise inaccessible and following ancient routes. Vegetarian food and sleeping bags are provided, as well as English-speaking guides. Jeep tours also available.

From Sharahut it is also possible to hike to Yotvata, if you are feeling particularly adventurous; you will need maps, overnight equipment, a lot of water and the advice of locals.

Khan Aviran, Peran, T08-6581821/052-3868938, www.han-aviran.co.il. Hire a 4WD plus guide, or take a guided hike. Tours are tailored to suit each group/individuals (from low-key half-day tours with kids, to extreme full-day treks). Amos will sort you out: he's an expert in the region and knows all the canyons and trails. He is also happy to give advice to those who are doing it alone.
Kibbutz Lotan, www.kibbutzlotan.com, can arrange guided nature trails in 6 languages, and birding tours during the spring and autumn migrations, for half-day or longer.
Watsu, Kibbutz Lotan, www.kibbutzlotan. com. Shiatsu in water within a self-constructed building. Individual (50 mins, 210NIS) and family sessions available, plus 6-day courses.

Dead Sea

Arriving at the Dead Sea

The Dead Sea Region is linked via Route 90 (then Route 1) to Jerusalem to the northwest, and by Route 90 to Eilat to the south. Although the main sites have good bus connections to Jerusalem (1½ hours) or Eilat (two to three hours), travelling around the Dead Sea region itself by public transport requires some advanced planning. Of course, a hired car is the ideal way to explore the region. Those on a tighter budget may like to try one of the day package tours organized from Jerusalem, although these provide only very limited time at each spot.

It should be noted that most of the accommodation in the region is in the upper-end price categories, with the cheapest options being the camps in Ne'ot HaKikar or youth hostels at Ein Gedi and Masada.

Background

Despite the seemingly inhospitable nature of the Dead Sea region, there is in fact a long record of human activity in the surrounding area. The history of the Dead Sea region is very closely intertwined with the history of the Judean Desert that lays to the northwest and west. Human occupation along the shores of the Dead Sea did not end with God's destruction of Sodom and Gomorrah (*Genesis 18, 19*).

The region has primarily been seen as both a place of refuge and as a centre for commercial exploitation. The Dead Sea Works that was established here by the British in 1930 is merely a continuation of a process of commercial exploitation that may have begun almost 2500 years ago with the Nabateans, who sold the surface bitumen to the Egyptians for use in the embalming business, an industry that continued well into Roman times. Whilst the Dead Sea Works continue to produce significant quantities of potash, bromine, magnesium, chloride and salts (as well as being an important employer of residents of towns such as Dimona), the Dead Sea region increasingly looks towards tourism as its major source of revenue and employment. But once again, like the industrial exploitation of the Dead Sea's resources, this is not a new phenomenon. A great deal of the Dead Sea's tourism industry is geared towards the apparent 'health and beauty' potential of the local environment. Much is made of the increased oxygen in the air (a function of the Dead Sea's position vis-à-vis sea level), the pollution-free environment (if you ignore the Dead Sea works!), and the medicinal properties of the various bromine, magnesium, iodine and mud treatments. Yet, as stressed before, this idea of the Dead Sea region as a 'refuge' from the rigours of the modern world is not new. Communities of hermits and ascetics (possibly including groups such as Essenes or individuals like John the Baptist) appear to have sought refuge in the region over 2000 years ago, in addition to political refugees who include amongst their number King David, Herod the Great and the Jewish Zealots (at Masada and possibly Qumran). Thus the fat old men and women who jostle you for position in the Ein Gedi Spa may be the latest link in a chain that began three millennia ago with King David.

Northern Dead Sea beaches

Arriving in the Northern Dead Sea beaches
These beaches are located 2 km off Road 90, shortly after 90 heads south along the Dead Sea. Egged buses 444/486/487 stop at Kalia Jct, be sure to tell the driver where you want to get off. It's about a 2-km walk from the bus stop.

Past the rusting remains of a failed water park and the empty shells of a Jordanian village, north of Qumran, are three beaches that can be visited for the day or overnight. The shore here is mud (don't imagine golden sand) and part of the experience is smearing it all over yourself. Bring a towel, as this is not included in entrance fees for day visitors. During the week these beaches are popular with Palestinians, while at the weekend Israelis tend to take over.

New Kalia Beach ① *T02-9942391, adults 40NIS, student/child 30NIS, summer 0730-1700, winter 0800-1600*, is the first you come to and has perhaps the nicest beach area. There's good shade, a snack-bar, a shop selling Dead Sea products and the "lowest bar in the world" at -418 m. It's generally just for day visits, although groups of 20 can be accommodated in a tent.

Next along is **Biankini** ① *Siesta Beach, T02-9400266/050-7616162, biankini1@walla.co.il, entry 50NIS per day*. Here you'll find a Moroccan kasbah with three apartments sleeping up to six people, 21 (and expanding) colourful and well-equipped chalets with jacuzzis (ask for one with view, much preferable, 650/750NIS per couple B&B week/weekend) and a tent sleeping up to 50 (100NIS per person). Those turning up after 1600 with a tent can sleep for 50NIS each. Beach is small but well-maintained, restaurant serves 26 kinds of tagine (45-49NIS, can feed two people) plus ethnic salads and dairy menu. The enormous outdoor terrace is a fine location overlooking the Dead Sea, food is served 0800-2400 (winter -2000).

Next door (but cut off by a fence) is **Neve Midbar** ① *T02-9942781, www.nevemidbar-beach.com, day entry 35NIS, overnight with a tent 50NIS per person*, where there is a Middle Eastern restaurant and accommodation in the form of 'husha' huts (190NIS per couple) that have mattresses and no more. The beach is open to day visitors 0800-1900 (winter 0800-1800). The camping spot overlooking the water is ideal, there's a bar, and sand has been imported to make the top beach more appealing.

Qumran

Though this site is rather unprepossessing, its significance derives from the fact that this is where most of the Dead Sea Scrolls were discovered (see box, page 107). There are few sites in Israel/Palestine that create more controversy and ill-feeling between theologians, archaeologists and historians than Qumran, yet few issues surrounding the site and the treasures found here have been satisfactorily resolved. For example, there is still ferocious debate with regard to the date of the founding of the community, the nature of the community settled here, their period of occupation, their reason for abandoning the site, and the date that the occupation finished. In fact, every single aspect of life at Qumran!

Arriving in Qumran
Getting there and away Most visitors come as part of a tour. All buses between Jerusalem and Ein Gedi, Masada, Eilat etc on Route 90 stop opposite the turning to the site (five-minute walk uphill), though you should take care to remind the driver to stop. Qumran is also accessible by service taxi from Jericho. For bus timings, see entries under the destinations mentioned above.

Getting around The compact nature of the site, and the fact that it is clearly labelled, means that a detailed tour description is not necessary. A short film starts a visit, followed by the small museum and then the archaeological remains outside. **Note** It is not possible to explore many of the caves in which the Dead Sea Scrolls were found. Cave 6 to the northwest is the most readily accessible, whilst Cave 4 is clearly visible in the cliff face across the ravine from the observation point. There is no fee for trekking in the Qumran National Park. It's possible to ramble around the hills (about 30 minutes to the top) or follow a trail to En Feshka (around five hours). Get hiking advice from staff at the entrance kiosk, where you can also check that there is no danger of flash floods (if so, paths are closed off).

The site
ⓘ *T02-9942235. Daily 0800-1700, winter 0800-1600, closes 1 hr earlier on Fri and hol eves. Adult 21NIS, student 18NIS, child 9NIS, combined ticket with Einot Tzukim 36NIS. Huge souvenir shop, toilets, restaurant.*

The 'consensus' view has long been that Qumran was occupied by a Jewish breakaway group referred to as the Essenes. This sect, or sub-sect, of Judaism is generally characterized as celibate, ascetic, reclusive, pacifist, and divorced from the mainstream of religious, political and social thought; hence Qumran would appear to be a perfect location for such

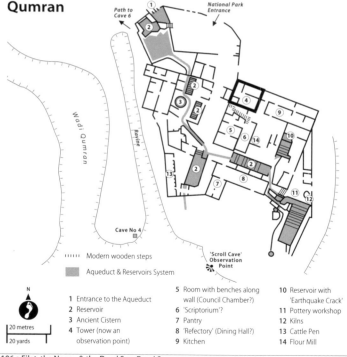

Qumran

Path to Cave 6

National Park Entrance

Wadi Qumran

Ravine

Cave No 4

ıııııı Modern wooden steps

▨ Aqueduct & Reservoirs System

'Scroll Cave' Observation Point

N
20 metres
20 yards

1 Entrance to the Aqueduct
2 Reservoir
3 Ancient Cistern
4 Tower (now an observation point)
5 Room with benches along wall (Council Chamber?)
6 'Scriptorium'?
7 Pantry
8 'Refectory' (Dining Hall?)
9 Kitchen
10 Reservoir with 'Earthquake Crack'
11 Pottery workshop
12 Kilns
13 Cattle Pen
14 Flour Mill

The Dead Sea Scrolls

A chance discovery in 1947 by a young Bedouin shepherd boy, Mohammad adh-Dhib of the Ta'amireh tribe, became one of the greatest archaeological finds of this century. Whilst searching for a stray goat in caves on the northwest shore of the Dead Sea, adh-Dhib came across a number of earthenware jars containing leather scrolls wrapped in linen. Once it became apparent that something of value had been found here, a series of excavations and bounty-hunting expeditions began (though it's difficult to distinguish between the archaeologists and the Bedouins as to who were the bigger trophy-hunters). A veritable corpus of material has now been gathered from caves in the region, much of it in fragments, but other sections, such as the 'Isaiah Scroll' being several metres long. Most of the material has been divided into two broad categories, 'religious' and 'secular', though most scholars now consider the latter category as more interesting (and controversial) since it seems to indicate much about the community at Qumran and elsewhere.

a group. Such an image of the Essenes is derived from their depiction in the works of Josephus, Philo and Pliny, with the inference being that they closely resemble the modern idea of a monastic order.

This image has been challenged over the years by a number of commentators (most spectacularly Baigent and Leigh), who question the 'Qumran-Essene Hypothesis' on a number of points. For example, if the community here were celibate, why are there graves of women and children in Qumran's main burial ground? And why is there no reference to the term 'Essene' in the Dead Sea Scrolls? In fact, some scholars argue that the scrolls may have had nothing to do with the community living at Qumran itself, but were merely placed in the caves for safe-keeping by rebels fleeing from the Romans during the First Revolt (66-70 CE). They were not written here, but brought from the Temple and libraries of Jerusalem. It has also been hypothesized that the glassware and range of coinage discovered points to a community concerned with worldly matters of trade and commerce, and not with sectarian religiosity. The latest controversial view is that of Prof Rachel Elior, who doubts the very existence of the Essenes as a group, postulating that the sect was invented by Josephus and that the scrolls were written by a class of Jerusalem priests banished from the Temple in the second century BCE.

There are no clear answers. However, if it proves nothing else, the argument over Qumran shows how open to interpretation the field of archaeology is. When visiting the site of Qumran, you will find the community are now often referred to as 'Yahad' ('together' in Hebrew) or perhaps as the.'Sect of the Wilderness of Judea', rather than simply as Essenes.

Make sure you go to the viewpoint to look over the caves, or even take a walk in the hills of the National Park. The restaurant in the visitors' complex is acceptable, with buffet meals at not too ridiculous prices (eg main course, soup and salad for 60NIS).

En Feshka (Einot Tzukim) Nature Reserve

① T02-9942355. Daily 0800-1700, winter 0800-1600, closes 1 hr earlier on Fri and hol eves. Adult 27NIS, child 14NIS, combination ticket with Qumran adult 36NIS. Snack shop, toilets, picnic areas, BBQs. Buses stop next to the reserve entrance.

This oasis features a series of winding streams and pools amongst the reeds and trees, and is unique in having natural freshwater bathing spots so close to the Dead Sea. However, as signs indicate, the waters are not as close as they used to be – staff at the reserve will explain the frightening recession of the northern Dead Sea. There are short walks though the rushes, a swimming pool at weekends and a number of ruins from the Second Temple period (where balsam was produced) which are not hugely impressive but worth a look. To protect flora and fauna, the southern part of the reserve can only be visited at weekends and it's best to time a visit to coincide with a **tour** *① Sep-Jun Fri at 1000 and 1200, and Sat 1000, 1200 and 1400, about 1 hr, included in entrance fee to park, in Hebrew but concessions made for English speakers.* In any case, the wading pools and scenic setting make for a refreshing stop.

Metzoke Dragot

Metzoke Dragot perches at the top of the Dead Sea cliffs, a dramatic drive up a snaking road that finishes in awe-inspiring views. There is a centre for 'adventure desert tourism' in the area, although activities are only offered to groups of 10 or more these days. However, should that apply, two-day rock-climbing, abseiling and rescue courses cost 680NIS per person, not including accommodation (contact T02-9944777). **Note** The centre does not give advice about trekking, contact T*3639 for advice, and for a contact for tours and rappelling (abseiling) see What to do, below. The main reason to come up here is for the stunning view and to spend a night at the guesthouse (see below). This area is also the home of the Wadi Murabba'at Caves, where a number of important artefacts have been found. The turning is 17 km south of Ein Feshka along Route 90 (signposted). Any bus between Jerusalem and Eilat will drop you at the turning (give the driver plenty of warning), although it is at least a one-hour walk uphill – you will probably want to hitch.

Ahava Visitors' Centre and Mineral Beach

A couple of kilometres south of the turning to Metzoke Dragot, you will see signs for the Ahava Visitors' Centre. If you are keen on the much-vaunted Ahava products, you might pick up a good deal in the **showroom** *① T02-9945117, Sun-Thu 0800-1700, Fri 0800-1600, Sat and hols 0830-1700.* There is also an information centre, with a presentation explaining production methods, and a coffee bar.

Mineral Beach *① T02-9944888, www.dead-sea.co.il, winter 0900-1700 mid-week 0800-1700, weekend, summer and hols add 1 hr, entry 45NIS mid-week, 55NIS weekends,* provides good access to the Dead Sea, as well as café, beach bar and freshwater and hot sulphur pools. Entrance to the beach is free with a 50- or 80-minute massage (prices from 220-370NIS depending on massage type/length/day of week!). It's a fair deal for the facilities on offer, especially when compared to other beaches in the northern Dead Sea and at Ein Boqeq.

For hotel and restaurant price codes and other relevant information, see pages 12-16.

Where to stay
Metzoke Dragot Desert Village,
T08-6223012, www.metzoke.co.il. Truly outstanding views of the Dead Sea with hills of Jordan reflected in the glassy waters. This 'resort' on the edge of the cliff is rather like a holiday camp, with hammocks and seating dotted about. Basic rooms are small and featureless, but clean and have a/c – still expensive for what you get at 400-600NIS including breakfast (depending on season/no of persons/type of room); some renovated rooms have fridge, kettle, storage, new showers. Also 6 Bedouin tents can sleep 50-100 people in each. Essential to book in advance, frequently taken by groups, mattress only – bring a sleeping bag (adults 60NIS, child 40NIS). Restaurant serves dinner at weekends or by arrangement for groups, and there's a small coffeeshop/bar.

What to do
Gyora Eldar, T052-3971774, eldarara@017. net.il. Organizes rappelling and jeep tours in the Metzoke Dragot area.

Ein Gedi

Ein Gedi is a large oasis on the western shore of the Dead Sea, taking its name from a perennial spring that rises some 200 m above shore level. It was held as a biblical symbol of beauty (*Song of Solomon 1:14*), retaining that image today as a vibrant splash of greenery, rich vegetation, pools and waterscapes amongst the austere hills of the Judean Desert and the sterile depths of the Dead Sea. The Ein Gedi Nature Reserve includes the excellent hiking trails around Wadi David and Wadi 'Arugot, one of the Dead Sea's best-established bathing beaches (Ein Gedi Beach), and a health and beauty resort providing therapeutic bathing (Ein Gedi Spa). There are also a number of accommodation options, which make Ein Gedi a good spot from which to explore the Dead Sea Region.

Arriving in Ein Gedi
Getting there and away The Ein Gedi region is accessible by bus from Jerusalem, Eilat, Arad and Be'er Sheva (see page 114 for timings), although many visitors come on a day trip that does not really do justice to the region.

Getting around Getting between the various sites is a bit of a pain without your own transport, as buses are a bit too infrequent to make them practical.

Background
The most celebrated story concerning Ein Gedi recalls David's flight from Saul, when he sought sanctuary in the "wilderness of En-gedi" (*I Samuel 24:1*). David passed up the opportunity to kill Saul when the latter went into a cave to "cover his feet" (*I Samuel 24:3*), ie take a dump. David chose instead to prostate himself at Saul's feet (after he'd finished his business), leading to the reconciliation of the two. There is significant evidence of settlement throughout the region in the Chalcolithic period (4500-3300 BCE), most notably at the Chalcolithic temple above Wadi David, whilst En-Gedi is listed amongst the wilderness cities of Judah (*Joshua 15:62*) prior to reaching its fame during Saul's reign (c.1020-1004 BCE).

In later years it is mentioned by Josephus in the context of raids by the Sicarii during the First Jewish Revolt (66-73 CE, see *Jewish War IV, 402*), with documents found in the

Sinkholes

The parched landscape of the Dead Sea has evolved some new features in recent years, making it even further resemble the surface of the moon. About 3000 craters have opened along the shoreline – sinkholes, which as the name implies, pose a physical as well as environmental hazard.

It's not unknown for an unwary hiker to plunge down a hole or for the ground to open up and swallow a building. Warning signs and fenced off areas now dot sections of the coast, and it is wise to heed them. The problem is concentrated in the northern lake – the sinkholes are clearly visible from the road as you travel between Ein Feshkha and Masada.

Also found on the Jordanian side, sinkholes are a direct result of the receding water levels. This leaves a layer of subterranean salt at the newly exposed shoreline, which then gets dissolved by fresh water coming in. Thus a hole can form underground and, when it collapses in on itself, whatever lies above has to take its chances.

Who knows how many more lie below the surface? This is surely one more reason for governments to reconsider the constant draining of the water supply to the Dead Sea.

Cave of Letters in Nahal Hever to the south suggesting that it was also a centre of Jewish activity during the Bar Kokhba Revolt (132-136 CE). Ein Gedi remained a large Jewish village cultivating dates and balsam-producing plants throughout the Byzantine period, though subsequent occupation has been far more intermittent.

Ein Gedi Nature Reserve

① *T08-6584285, www.parks.org.il. Daily 0800-1700, winter 0800-1600. Adult 27NIS, student 21NIS, child 14NIS; synagogue only 14NIS, child 7NIS, ticket valid for 1 day. The leaflet for the site contains good information and further choices of hikes to those given here. Snack bar, drinking water and toilets at the entrance.*

Many people spend insufficient time here and end up following the hordes of visitors who pop in, head up to **David Falls** (15 minutes), continue to **Dodim Cave** (40 minutes), head up to the Chalcolithic temple (10 minutes), on to **Ein Gedi Spring** (five minutes), and then leave again after little more than an hour. If you come on one of the 'see the Dead Sea in one day' type tours, this is what you will end up doing, though for those with children or unable to walk long distances this will probably be enough. If you can spare the time, base yourself locally and spend four to six hours on the **Dry Canyon hike** that takes in all the main sites and gets you away from the crowds. **Note** This hike is not suitable for all, and involves some steep ascents and descents. Do not forget to bring plenty of drinking water, but not food: it is forbidden to eat within the reserve. Sightings of Nubian ibex and Syrian hyraxes are more than common.

Dry canyon hike

This hike begins at the SPNI Field School (**2**) above the Ein Gedi Youth Hostel (**1**). Follow the road up to the small amphitheatre and exit through the gate in the fence. There is nobody here to collect your admission fee. Follow the black trail in a steep upwards direction (it is signposted 'Ma'ale Har Yishay'). After a short distance the trail divides, with the black trail continuing up to Har Yishay to the right (at least one hour), and the red trail continuing straight ahead. Follow the red trail towards the 4-m-high cliff (**3**), and continue up it. After ascending the low cliff, take the lower path to your left towards the edge of the cliff above the Nahal David canyon. Continue along the path above Nahal David and David Falls (which you can hear below) until you reach a small gully (4). Drop down into the gully and follow it round to the left where it enters the **dry canyon** above the Nahal David. **Note** Do not enter this canyon if there is the slightest possibility of rain, since it is subject to flash-floods. Also note that the rocks in this canyon have been worn treacherously slippery by water action.

Not far into the dry canyon, shortly after it has become steeper and narrower, a number of metal stakes have been hammered into the rock to your right (5) to show you the route out of the canyon, and to assist your ascent. Climb the metal stakes back out of the canyon to the south. You soon hit a green trail running parallel to the dry canyon. Follow it to the left (southeast), and then continue to the top of the small hill in front of you. The hill looks down upon the whole Ein Gedi area, with the **Chalcolithic temple** (6) below you. Remains found at the temple include a clay statuette of a laden bull, animal bones, horns and pottery. Follow the path down from the Chalcolithic temple, taking the right (south) at the trail intersection (7) to **Ein Gedi Spring** (8). The spring provides welcome relief on a hot day, though it has to

Wadi David (including the 'dry canyon hike')

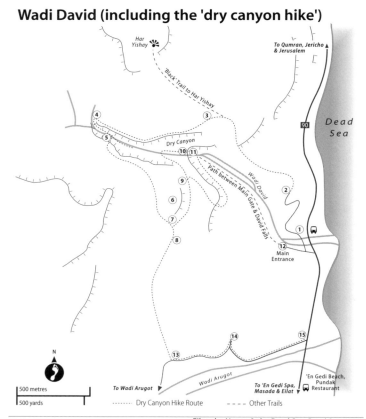

Map legend:
- .... Dry Canyon Hike Route
- ‒ ‒ ‒ Other Trails

500 metres
500 yards

To Wadi Arugot ▼

Wadi Arugot

To 'En Gedi Spa, Masada & Eilat ▼

'En Gedi Beach, Pundak Restaurant

'Swimming' in the Dead Sea

With a salt concentration of over 20%, the Dead Sea actually supports one's body on the surface, and prevents 'swimming' as such: 'floating' is a far more accurate description. Before taking the almost obligatory dip in the Dead Sea, bear these points in mind: Firstly, it is best to use one of the recognized 'beaches' since these have fresh-water showers that allow you to wash off the residue that is left on your skin after bathing. Secondly, avoid getting water in your eyes since it will sting like hell and may cause inflammation. If you do get water in your eyes, rinse immediately and continuously with fresh water. For this reason, noticeboards at the beaches outlaw splashing. Thirdly, the water of the Dead Sea also tastes extremely unpleasant, and may make you feel sick if swallowed. Lastly, the salty water causes agony in every minute scratch and cut; shaving prior to a dip in the sea is really not advisable.

Because floating in the Dead Sea is such an unusual experience, it is not recommended that you attempt to lie on your front in the water; flicking yourself over on to your back is not as easy as it sounds, and might be a cue to splash water in your eyes/mouth. In fact most of the beaches have noticeboards giving information on how to get into the water (walk backwards and then assume a sitting position). Children should be supervised, with the 'ground-rules' carefully explained to them.

be noted that it is only mid-shin deep, and is impossibly crowded if more than five people are gathered here. There are several options from here: i) Continue south along the trail, taking in Tel Goren (**13**) and the Ancient Synagogue (**14**), before returning to Route 90 (15) at a point 500 m south of the Youth Hostel (1); ii) Follow the loop trail to the north, visiting Dodim Cave (**10**), then David Falls (**11**), before exiting the Nature Reserve at the main gate (**12**); iii) Visiting Dodim Cave (**10**) and David Falls (**11**) as described in option ii), then returning to Ein Gedi Spring (**8**) to pursue option i). The route described here follows option iii).

Head north from Ein Gedi Spring, taking the right fork at the intersection (**7**), and passing beneath the ledge upon which the Chalcolithic temple stands (6). After several minutes walking, you reach another trail intersection (**9**). To visit the Dodim Cave take the signposted trail down to your left. Leopards are said to inhabit this area occasionally, though it is extremely unlikely that you will meet any. You are likely to come across ibex here, though, whose rustling in the reeds may scare the life out of you. The trail soon reaches the banks of Nahal David, though it is forbidden to follow it up to its source for fear of disturbing the flora and fauna. Note above you the 'mouth' of Window Falls. Descend to Nahal David using a series of ladders-cum-steps cut from the rock, before crossing the stream. Follow the path along the north bank to a large boulder. On the path below you it is possible to see swarms of visitors making their way up to David Falls. To reach Dodim Cave (**10**) (sometimes called Shulamit Cave), climb down the series of metal steps and grab rails. Unless you climb down (there are two separate ladders), the cave is largely hidden, though a full descent really means getting wet in the lovely pool here.

From here, retrace your steps to the intersection (**9**), then follow the path in a loop round to **David Falls** (**11**). Though the streams and falls here are very pleasant, unless you're very lucky this section of the Nature Reserve tends to be very busy. From David Falls you can either follow the path back to the main entrance (**12**), or climb back up to the intersection (**9**) to return to Ein Gedi Spring (**8**) and continue the tour.

From Ein Gedi Spring, follow the sign for 'Tel Goren' heading south. Though the low mound of Tel Goren (**13**) is not terribly impressive, five levels of occupation have been identified here, dating from the first Israelite settlement in the seventh century CE to the Late Roman and Byzantine periods (second to sixth century CE).

Beyond Tel Goren is the exit to the Nahal David Nature Reserve, where you hit the surfaced road. A right turn (west) here leads to Wadi Arugot (see below), whilst by following the road to the left (east) you soon come to the **Ancient Synagogue** (**14**) (separate entrance fee) which has its mosaic floor intact.

From the Ancient Synagogue, follow the paved road until it hits the main road, Route 90 (**15**). From here it is approximately 500 m back to the Youth Hostel (**1**).

Wadi Arugot
ⓘ *The entrance is about 2 km along the turn-off from Route 90, 1 km south of the Ein Gedi Youth Hostel. Oct-Mar, last entrance 1400.*
Less famous than its neighbour, Wadi Arugot receives far fewer visitors than Wadi David, and it is easier to get away from the crowds. The most popular walk is up to the Hidden Waterfall, one to 1½ hours from the entrance (follow the marked trail along the stream), though you can continue up to the Upper Pools (about another 30 minutes).

Ein Gedi Beach
The main (though not necessarily the best) bathing spot in the northern Dead Sea Region is the Ein Gedi Beach, a little over 1 km south of the Ein Gedi Youth Hostel. The beach is rather stony and unattractive, but has changing rooms, toilets, umbrellas and freshwater showers. A lifeguard is on duty 0800-1600. **Note** Keep an eye on your possessions whilst bathing here. The **Pundak Ein Gedi Restaurant** ⓘ *1000-1800, including Sat and hols,* offers kosher bland cafeteria-style food (eg schnitzel and chips) in an equally bland environment, though everything is fresh. There is also a 24-hour snack-bar on the beach. There's a bus stop at the beach; for onward travel, see below (though you will have to add or subtract five minutes or so).

Kibbutz Ein Gedi
Kibbutz Ein Gedi is located about 1.5 km off Route 90 and about 1.5 km south of Ein Gedi Beach. Though agriculture plays a large part in the economy of the kibbutz, it is sustained through tourism (most notably through the hotel it runs, see below). The **Botanical Gardens** ⓘ *T08-6584444, daily 0830-1600, Fri 0830-1400, adult 25NIS, student/child 22NIS, (free for guests at the kibbutz hotel). Night tours on Tue/Thu at 2000, individuals phone ahead to book with credit card*, here are really something special. There are over 800 rare species of plant from all over the globe thriving in the desert air, including exotic rainforest plants alongside Biblical frankincense and myrrh. However, it's the cacti collection that really catches the eye: towering examples of these flourish all over the kibbutz.

Ein Gedi Hot Springs and Spa
ⓘ *T08-6594934, Sun-Fri adults 69NIS, students 55NIS, Sat 79/63NIS, entrance plus lunch deal 110NIS. Sat-Thu 0800-1800, winter 0800-1600,closes 1 hr earlier on Fri.*
Four kilometres south of the turning for Kibbutz Ein Gedi is the Ein Gedi Spa. The spa offers the famed Dead Sea black mud and natural minerals treatments, as well as therapeutic bathing in sulphurous pools, massages and a (seasonal) freshwater swimming pool. Now that the waters of the Dead Sea have receded so far, a trolley is necessary to ferry clients

more than 1 km down to the shore. Twenty-five years ago when it was built, the spa was on the lakeshore. Facilities are free for guests of the Country Hotel. There's a bus stop at the spa; for onward travel see below (though you will have to add or subtract five minutes or so).

Ein Gedi listings

For hotel and restaurant price codes and other relevant information, see pages 12-16.

Where to stay and restaurants
$$$ Ein Gedi Country Hotel, Kibbutz Ein Gedi, T08-6594220/1/2, www.ein-gedi. co.il. Standard or deluxe rooms in a rural setting. All mod-cons. Most pleasing are the standard 'Desert Rooms' decorated by local artists. Accommodation is half-board only, and includes free entrance to Ein Gedi Spa. Relaxing on the grass by their big beautiful pool on the edge of a cliff above the Dead Sea is as good as it gets. Wellness Centre has Ayurvedic treatments. The 'Botanical Garden' restaurant has a good spread of Middle Eastern-Mediterranean cuisine, buffet-style (non-guests welcome, but phone in advance, daily 0700-1000, 1230-1400 and 1830-2100). There is also a pleasant bar and café area.
$$-$ IYHA Beit Sarah Ein Gedi Youth Hostel, T02-5945600, www.iyha.co.il. With a wonderful setting, rooms are also a step up from your typical hostel. Dorms rooms all have TV, a/c, tea/coffee (120NIS), roomy doubles, some have balconies with views (400NIS). Breakfast included, meals available, cafeteria, free Wi-Fi, basketball, 10 mins' walk to the Dead Sea. Enormous though the guesthouse is, it's necessary to book as far in advance as possible.

$$-$ SPNI Field School, T08-6584288. The first of Israel's field schools, founded in 1959, has great views over the Dead Sea and also into the National Park. Simple rooms but entirely adequate, for space in 5-bed a/c dorm it's 99NIS including breakfast, 74NIS without (women separate). Private doubles are 365NIS including breakfast. Advance booking definitely recommended. Fri night dinner available.

Transport
Although the bus times given here may change during the lifespan of this book, they give some idea as to the frequency of services. The timetables are usually posted at the Youth Hostel reception, or check with staff. All the buses heading south stop at **Ein Gedi Spa**, **Masada Junction** (2.6 km from Masada, with some continuing to the site itself) and **'Ein Boqeq**.

To **Arad** and Be'er Sheva: Bus 384, Sun-Thu 0800, 1230, 1530, 1800, Fri 0800, 1230. **Eilat** (via Masada, 'Ein Boqeq and Arava Rd): Bus 444, Sun-Thu 0800, 1100, 1500, 1800, Fri same but last at 1500, Sat 0100. **Jerusalem**: Buses 427/444/486/487, depart every couple of hrs, Sun-Thu 0600-1930, Fri same but last at 1415, Sat 1900, 1945, 0045. Add or subtract about 5 mins if catching the bus at Ein Gedi Beach, Kibbutz Ein Gedi or Ein Gedi Spa.

Ein Gedi to Masada

Approximately 7 km south of Ein Gedi the **Nahal Hever**, one of the deepest canyons in the Judean Desert, drains into the Dead Sea. During the Bar Kokhba Revolt (132-136 CE), Jewish fighters sought refuge from the Romans in the deep caves on both sides of Nahal Hever's valley. Two caves in particular have revealed priceless remains, artefacts and documents. The **Cave of Horrors** revealed the skeletons of 40 men, women and children who had been starved to death by the Roman siege of the cave. In the nearby **Cave of**

Letters archaeologists discovered an 'archive of Babata' and 'Bar Kokhba Letters'. Neither cave is accessible to visitors.

A further 6 km south on Route 90, one of the longest canyons in the Judean Desert, **Nahal Ze'elim**, flows into the Dead Sea. A number of caves in this valley revealed items from the Chalcolithic (4500-3300 BCE), Iron Age II (1000-586 BCE) and Bar Kokhba (132-136 CE) periods.

Masada

The high fortress at Masada must be one of the greatest and most exciting viewpoints in the Middle East, overlooking vast areas of the Dead Sea/Rift Valley and the Jordanian Heights. Yet Masada is more than just a spectacular location. The extensive excavations carried out have confirmed as fact much of the Jewish historian Josephus' account of the extraordinary events here in the first century CE. As the last outpost of resistance in the Jewish Revolt of 66-73 CE, it was here that 967 Jewish rebels preferred mass suicide to submission to Rome. Today, Masada is one of Israel's most visited archaeological sites, though within the Israeli psyche Masada represents far more than just an ancient place of archaeological interest. Many visitors to Masada take advantage of the early opening hours (0430) to climb to the top so that they can watch the sun rise over the Dead Sea and the Jordanian Heights. A truly magical experience. It is an easier (and shorter) climb in the dark from the western side than from the main entrance on the east. It is advisable to bring warm clothes since it can be rather cold waiting for the sun, even in summer.

Arriving in Masada

Getting there and away   Masada is located just off Route 90, around 18 km south of Ein Gedi and 15 km north of 'Ein Boqeq. Some of the buses between Jerusalem and Eilat (via Ein Gedi) take you all the way to the site, whilst others will only drop you at the turn-off (from where it's 2.6 km to the site). Make sure that the driver knows you want to get off at Masada.

Getting around   The fortress has immense natural barriers, and land access is possible only by two steep paths. Most visitors take the cable-car both up and down (and this is advisable for the very young or old). It is a taxing 45-minute step climb up the Snake Path from the main east entrance, a real killer in the heat (the path is in fact closed, going up, from 1000). Walking up the western Roman ramp takes 15 to 20 minutes and is a more gradual and shorter ascent.

Background

The main written historical sources on Masada are the works of Josephus (*Antiquities; The Jewish War*), though like everything else from this source, a healthy degree of scepticism is required when examining details. There still remains some doubt as to the nature of the site here during the Hasmonean period, and things only become clearer during the Herodian era.

Most of the remains seen today at Masada date to the reign of **Herod the Great** (37 BCE-4 BCE), though some structures were certainly built later by the rebels. Herod's association with Masada began in 40 BCE, when he was fleeing with his family from the pretender Antigonus and the Parthian army. Herod's brother Joseph, with 800 men, resisted Antigonus' siege, though they are only said to have survived dying of thirst by a fortuitous cloud-burst that filled the rock-cut cisterns on the summit. When Herod returned from Rome in 39 BCE, he rescued his family and then set about adding to Masada's considerable natural defences. It should be noted that Herod viewed Masada as less of a strategic stronghold protecting his kingdom, and more as a place of refuge for himself.

Access to the 'Roman Ramp' entrance to Masada

The western entrance to the fortress at Masada, (the 'Roman Ramp'), is accessible by vehicle only from Arad (though there is no public transport to the site). The west side of Masada is also the venue for the Son et Lumière (Sound and Light) show. The Roman Ramp entrance is 20 km northeast of Arad, along Route 3199. To reach Route 3199, head along Moav to the eastern limits of Arad, before turning left on to Tzur just before the *Margoa Arad Hotel*. Masada is then signposted along the road to the right (northeast). It's an awe-inspiring drive in the late afternoon light.

Masada's history subsequent to Herod's death in 4 BCE is unclear, though it was certainly occupied by a Roman garrison at the outbreak of the Jewish Revolt in 66 CE. Though Josephus does not give details, Masada was captured 'by stealth' by the Jews, and its Roman garrison exterminated (*Jewish War, II*, 408). It subsequently became a refuge for the duration of the Revolt, ruled by the 'tyrant' or 'autocrat' **Eleazar ben Yair**. Joined by other groups fleeing Jerusalem in 70 CE after the destruction of the Temple, the rebels increased the level of fortification at Masada (72-73 CE) and held out against a 6000-8000 man Roman army for two years. It took the construction of a massive ramp up the western slope of the mountain for the Romans to gain entry by force. Eventually it became obvious that the defences would be overwhelmed, as the outer Herodian stone wall was breached and then the inner wooden retaining walls were set on fire. The rebels made a decision to take their own lives, something expressly forbidden by Jewish law, rather than become slaves. So, after killing their wives and their families, 10 men were allocated the task of dispatching the others. Then one man was allotted the task of dispatching the remaining nine, before killing himself. Out of the rebel garrison estimated at nearly 1000 persons, when the Romans finally entered Masada they found only two women and five children alive, who had hidden in a water cistern. A section of Eleazar ben Yair's speech that incited the mass suicide, as reported by Josephus, is included in the free brochure and site plan that you are given upon entry to the National Park. It is generally believed that Josephus used considerable artistic licence in his account of Eleazar ben Yair's stirring words (some suggest that he made the entire thing up), though archaeology has largely confirmed the events that he outlined. Eleven small ostraca discovered close to the Water Gate may even contain the original 'lots' that were cast to decide who should kill whom. These can be seen in the new museum (see page 118).

The site was occupied by a Roman garrison for some years after the siege and mass suicide of 73 CE, perhaps as late as 111 CE if the evidence of coinage found here is taken into consideration. Pottery finds have also suggested that Nabatean soldiers were included amongst the Roman siege troops and subsequent garrison. Christian monks occupied Masada during the fifth and sixth centuries CE, constructing a church and living as hermits on the summit. Following their demise, Masada appears to have been largely forgotten until being correctly identified by Robinson and Smith in 1838 (from Ein Gedi, via a telescope!).

The site

① *T08-4584207/8, www.parks.org.il. Daily sunrise-1700. By foot, adult 27NIS, student 21NIS, child 14NIS. Cable-car operates 0800-1700 (Fri 0800-1500) every 15 mins; one-way adult 54NIS, student 45NIS, child 27NIS; return adult 72NIS, student 63NIS, child 41NIS; price includes admission fee. Handheld audio-guide available in 6 languages, 20NIS (includes entrance to* the museum). There is a short film shown on a loop. Self-service cafeteria (fairly pricey, closes early), McDonalds, souvenirs, toilets at the bottom and top, (free) cold drinking water at the top. There is an official campsite on the western side (see page 119).

Viewed from the north, Masada is an enormous rock pinnacle standing out from the main ridges and peaks of the hills of the western Dead Sea coast. The site is separated from its surroundings on all sides by precipitous slopes: 120 m on the west where it connects to the hill range behind, 400 m on its northern and southern sides and more than 434 m on the coastal cliff. In addition, the approach to Masada from the west is through the bleak and poorly watered hills of Judea or from the east through the wilderness of the Wadi Arava. Both were difficult to penetrate and gave the site a unique strength, exploited in the Jewish revolts against Roman rule.

The site is well labelled so a detailed tour description in this *Handbook* is not necessary. However, some further details of the key places of interest are included below. If you want some peace and solitude head over to the southern side of the site, which few visitors bother exploring. **Note** The black line indicates the height of the walls found *in situ*, whilst construction above this line represents reconstruction made by archaeologists using masonry found scattered nearby.

The walls The great walls of Masada comprise the outer walls of the site built by the Romans during the siege of 72-73 AD, which straggle round the foot of the escarpments with garrison camps at intervals. On the heights is the main fortress wall with its 30 towers and bastions running for some 1400 m. It is constructed of two encasing limestone block walls infilled with rubble, giving an overall width of some four metres. The 70 or so rooms in the casement wall were used as living quarters by the Zealots and their families, and have revealed a large number of artefacts.

Northern Palace-Villa The most spectacular building on the site, and described in some detail by Josephus, it is built in three tiers on the northern edge of the cliff. The upper terrace comprised a semi-circular balcony with the living quarters to the south, whilst the middle terrace some 20 m below featured some form of entertainment complex. A further 15 m down is the lower terrace, where a central hall surrounded by porticoes also served some form of entertainment purpose. Remains of the sandstone columns, with fluted drums and Corinthian capitals, can still be seen, along with replicas of the decorative frescoes (originals are now in the museum). A small bathhouse stands to the east, the ultimate location for a sauna. During the period of the Revolt, the living quarters on the upper terrace retained their original function, whilst the lower levels were used as part of the strategic defence of the water source. A thick layer of ash suggests that the middle and lower terraces were consumed by fire, with remains from the Revolt including numerous arrowheads, plus the skeletons of a man, woman and child. The woman's scalp was complete with braids.

Western Palace The largest residential structure on Masada, covering almost 4000 sq m, the Western Palace served as the ceremonial and administrative centre. The royal apartments in the southeast contain several well-preserved mosaics, which should not be missed

The storehouses There appear to be two types of storehouses for food and weapons at Masada: public storehouses, and storehouses attached to specific buildings such as palaces and administrative centres. The largest **public storeroom complex** is located just to the south of the Northern Palace-Villa's upper terrace. It is believed that oil, wine, flour and other foodstuffs were each stored in separate rooms in special jars. Most of the storehouses containing foodstuffs were burnt at the climax of the siege, though some were left undamaged in order to prove to the Romans that the mass suicide was not a result of starvation.

The bathhouse This magnificent bathhouse comprises a large open court and four rooms: the *apodyterium* (entrance room), tepidarium (warm room), *frigidarium* (cold room) and the *caldarium* (hot room). The remains of the *hypocaust* (under-floor heating system) and *praefurnium* (furnace) are preserved. Immersion pools and *mikvehs* were added to many buildings during the period of the Revolt (66-73 CE), and the large bathhouse underwent significant alterations.

The water system The key element at Masada, at an elevation of over 400 m in the middle of a harsh desert, was the provision of water. The Israeli excavations have shown that the water system included setting up a water catchment to bring water to the vicinity of the fortress from the Ben Jair and Masada wadis, carried in places on aqueducts to storage pools. Water was stored in square cisterns, 4000 cu m in volume, cut into the rock: eight above and four below. Water was also carried to the site by animal and led to the cisterns by channels running from the Water Gate in the north of the fortress. Small scattered cisterns for storing rain water falling in the summit area were also in use and were important, if minor, supplies. The huge southern water cistern can be entered, via 64 steps, and gives a vivid picture of the vast water supplies that allowed the rebels to sustain themselves under siege for so long.

The Roman siege remains Outside the fortress are the structural remains of the Roman siege, led by Flavius Silva. In addition to the siege wall built to contain the site, there are clear signs of the Roman camps which were like fortified cities in themselves, with walls, towers and shops to accommodate the merchants who followed the Roman army. The extraordinary ramp built by the Roman general, close to the Western Gate, enabled a siege tower to destroy the entrance to the citadel. In all they are a memorial to the dedication of Flavius Silva to his task, and the effectiveness of Roman military engineering.

The Yigael Yadin Museum
ⓘ *Daily 0800-1600, entrance 20NIS, or free with a hand-held audio-guide.*
Billing it as 'an exciting museological experience' is a bit unnecessary, but this state-of-the-art museum is very worthwhile (perhaps best enjoyed after a visit to the summit when the dim cool interior is a relief). Most people don't bother with it, so a visit is peaceful and takes about 30 minutes. The sensor-activated guide gives a potted version of the information on the walls, from the time of Herod through to the Roman siege. Finds include the amphoras that brought exotic food and wines to Herod, gold jewellery and Jewish coins, a braid of hair found at the Northern Palace, belt buckles of the Roman soldiers and – most famous of all – the 'lots', perhaps those drawn to decide the fate of the rebels.

Sound and light show
ⓘ *Bookings through T08-9959333, rontal.n@npa.org.il. Performances take place Mar-Oct at 2100 on Tue and Thu, adult 45NIS, child 35NIS.*
Each Tuesday and Thursday a 50-minute sound and light show takes place at the amphitheatre by the Roman ramp (western) side of Masada. This is only accessible via Arad, from where travel time is about 30 minutes. The route is clearly signed along road 3199 from the west side of town. Aim to arrive at least half an hour before the performance

starts, as they shut the road when the show starts. Though commentary is in Hebrew, headphones provide simultaneous translation into English, French, German, Spanish or Russian. There is a cafeteria by the car park.

Masada listings

For hotel and restaurant price codes and other relevant information, see pages 12-16.

Where to stay and restaurants
See also Kfar Hanokdim, page 41, for accommodation on the west side of Masada.
$$$-$ IYHA Masada Youth Hostel/Isaac H Taylor Hostel, T08-9953222, www.iyha.org.il. Beautifully maintained hostel that resembles more of a hotel; a/c dorms with attached bath and TV (150NIS), or doubles (400NIS). Breakfast included, other meals order in advance, There's a great (seasonal) swimming pool, immense balcony-terrace, free Wi-Fi, safe. Advance reservations absolutely essential (ideally weeks in advance). On request, reception staff may separate those who are rising early to climb Masada from those after an undisturbed lie-in.
$ Masada Campsite, west side of Masada, T08-6280404, ext. 3. Toilets and showers, can pitch your own tent (adult/child 50/40NIS) or sleep in their big one (65/55NIS), There are cooking facilities, campfires are permitted, and the proximity to Masada when you wake up is a delight. Necessary to book in advance.

Transport
The bus times are posted on the window of the office next to the bus stop near Masada Youth Hostel. Note that all Jerusalem-bound services also stop at **Ein Gedi** and **Qumran**, whilst southbound services stop at **Ein Boqeq. Be'er Sheva** and **Arad**: Bus 384, Sun-Thu 0825, 1255, 1555, 1825, Fri 0825, 1255, 2 hrs. **Eilat**: Bus 444, Sun-Thu 0815, 1115, 1515, 1800, Fri same, last at 1513, 3 hrs. **Ein Gedi**: Sun-Thu about 10 per day, 0830-1915, Fri last at 1435, Sat 1845, 1923, 0023, 30 mins. **Jerusalem**: Buses 444/486, Sun-Thu, about 10 per day 0830-1950, Fri last at 1550, Sat 1815, 1920, 2 hrs. **Tel Aviv** (Arlozorov): Bus 421, Sun-Fri 1415, 3½ hrs.

Ein Boqeq

Ein Boqeq (Ein Bokek) is Israel's major tourist resort on the Dead Sea, where upmarket hotels provide private beaches, spas and health facilities. A couple of kilometres to the south at Hamme Zohar are three further hotels with spas, and the area between is mooted to be developed so that eventually the two will be linked.

Arriving in Ein Boqeq
Tourist information ⓘ *Tourist Office, Ein Boqeq 'Solarium -400', T08-9975010, www. deadsea.co.il, Mon-Thu 0900-1600, Fri 0900-1500.* Good spread of leaflets and flyers for the region, helpful staff.

Places in Ein Boqeq and what to do
The public beaches at Ein Boqeq are among the most attractive on the Dead Sea, though they can be prone to overcrowding. While there are no budget places to stay, the hotels all offer day use for their spas, swimming pools, heated Dead Sea water pools, saunas, jacuzzis and gyms. It's a good idea to browse and see which takes your fancy; prices almost always include lunch, massages cost (a lot) extra and use of sulphur pool costs 50-60NIS more. There are endless types of massage to chose from (180-650NIS, depending on type

and length), mud wraps 180-290NIS, hydro-baths 85NIS, facials 170-380NIS, body peeling 200-320NIS, plus various other weird and wonderful treatments.

Next to the 'Solarium -400' in the centre of Ein Boqeq is a stretch of public beach with free showers and sun-shades, toilets nearby (for changing) and no rocks underfoot. It is a fairly attractive spot with café-bars, mini-markets and a great ice cream parlour nearby – a good place for budget travellers to take a dip.

Mezad Boqeq and Officina
Ein Boqeq was probably first settled in the Hasmonean period (152-37 BCE), though its fame dates from the Herodian period (37 BCE-70 CE) when it became a centre for the manufacture of cosmetics and pharmaceuticals. A small Roman fort on the north side of the Wadi (Nahal) Boqeq valley was probably built as part of the Limes Palaestinae eastern frontier defences. A short section (2 m out of 1 km) of the **aqueduct** that served Ein Boqeq is visible to the northwest of the fort, as are two of the **cisterns** that stored water at the oasis. Less easy to find, to the east of the fort (nearer to the main Route 90), are the remains of the Herodian workshop, or **officina**. This building contained ovens, basins and vessels used in the perfume, cosmetic and pharmaceutical production process. It is speculated that raw materials such as buds, blossoms, seeds, fruits, resins, twigs, bark and leaves of aromatic plants were perhaps provided from the Far East and Arabia by the Nabatean trade caravans.

Wadi Boqeq Hike
This short hike brings you to fresh water pools – excellent respite from the heat of summer months and, unlike Ein Gedi Nature Reserve, entry is free (at least for now). Take flip flops, plenty of water, sun-screen and a hat. If driving, park by the Meridien David at the entrance to Ein Boqeq. Bus 444 stops on Route 90 at the start of the trek: disembark by the Meridien hotel.

From the Meridien, cross Route 90 (or go through the tunnel under the road from the hotel parking lot) and follow the brown sign to Ma'ale Boqeq a short way uphill, to where a signpost indicates 'Ma'ale Boqeq Ascent'. For a very short walk (that can be done in flip flops), turn left (south) here and head into the wadi (following the sign to Wadi Boqeq) where you pick up a black/white trail marker. After about 15 minutes' walking (either in the stream or alongside it) you will reach the first of two shallow pools of clean water, an excellent place to cool off and have a picnic. Only here and at Ein Gedi will you find freshwater pools all year round. For a longer alternative, at the signpost follow the red/white trail up the 'ascent'. Shortly you will pass Roman remains, then it's a steep climb uphill to meet a black marked trail going left along the ridge (the red trail continues up, but follow the black). Look out for ibex (Hebrew: 'yael') around here, they are a fairly common sight. A couple of minutes' walk, with the contradictory views of five-star hotels on the east side and the wild escarpment to the west, brings you to a descent into the rush-filled wadi. It's a steep, rocky path down, followed by a short vertical climb using metal rungs in the rock to water level. The clear stream leads to two shallow pools (separated by slippery steps); the second pool is deeper and more appealing for a dip. To reach this point takes about an hour. Then it's just 15 minutes back along the wadi bed to the Meridien hotel. The trail is marked with black/white throughout.

For hotel and restaurant price codes and other relevant information, see pages 12-16.

Where to stay

The 15 or so hotels in Ein Boqeq are much of a muchness, offering typical resort-style rooms with all the amenities you'd expect from a top-end hotel. Room rates tend to be grossly overpriced, although look online for deals. Note that in high season you need to book places 3-4 months in advance and at other times at least a week ahead.

$$$$ Daniel, T08-6689999, www.tamares hotels.co.il. Tasteful modern rooms (US$220/273 low/high season, plus US$59 for club level). Outdoor pool in a pleasant grassy area; spa has a smaller pool than some but feels less institutional, and is among the cheapest for day use at 100NIS. Castle pub has 1+1 on drinks 1900-2100, bowling alley. Not a bad option.

$$$$-$$$ Isrotel, T08-6689666, www.isrotel.com. Light, white contemporary lobby with rooms to match, smallish bathrooms, all have sea views from balcony. Private beach (across road), tennis, appealing circular 2-tier pool in landscaped surrounds, lovely spa but expensive for day use (though includes massage as well as lunch) which makes it less crowded for hotel guests. **Ranch House** restaurant for steaks.

$$$$-$$$ Lot Spa, T08-6689200, www.lothotel.co.il. Overpriced rooms, not all of which have sea views or balconies. It's the very attractive poolside area and excellent spa that is the draw here (day use 180NIS including lunch, no weekend price hikes). Turkish bath is 30NIS extra, lovely treatments area and treatments more reasonably priced than elsewhere. Next to the beach, bar by poolside, it can get exceedingly busy and attracts a younger clientele overall.

$$$$-$$$ Royal, T08-6688500, www.royalhoteldeadsea.com. Public areas not enormously flash, but rooms good for the price (especially by comparison): nice decor, balconies with side views of the Dead Sea; sofa, shower and bath. Day use at spa 150NIS. Feels a bit like the local swimming bath but is less packed out than other hotels. No weekend price rise.

$$$ Hod Hamidbar, T08-6688222, www.hodhotel.co.il. Exterior looking rather dated but, despite small balconies, rooms are pleasant and a fair size. Appealing sun deck around pool, it also benefits from being beach side of the road. One of the cheaper options in town for both rooms and spa, attracts the older clientele.

Restaurants

$$$ Sato Bistro, Crowne Plaza Hotel, T08-6591975. Quality Asian food. Reserve a table.

$$ Taj Mahal, by the pool at the Tulip Inn, T057-6506502, www.taj-mahal.co.il. Open 24 hrs. Not an Indian menu as you might suppose, but Middle Eastern/Western food in a Bedouin tent with well-stocked bar and nargilla (25NIS). If you eat here you can use the pool for free, and on Fri nights live music and belly-dancer from 2300. Go to website for 10% discount coupon.

$$-$ Aroma, Petra Centre. Daily 0800-2200. There's not much to choose from in the way of quick eats for those passing through, and this reliable café-chain does a good breakfast, excellent chicken sandwich, soups, and pints of beer. Wi-Fi, or lap-top on counter for customers to browse.

Also in the Petra Centre (located under the giant coffee cup and McDonalds arch) you will find ATMs, a minimarket (closed Shabbat) and money changers. Look out for Aldo's ice cream parlour near the public beach, which is recommended.

What to do

Pere Hamidbar, T08-9952711/050-3939394, s@jeeptours.co.il, www.jeeptours.co.il. Self-driving a low-slung mini-jeep (like a beefed-up golf buggy) along the wadis is loads of fun. They can traverse tracks only suitable for 4WDs, a guide will lead the way. US$100 per jeep (seats 4), minimum of 2 jeeps. Leave from

Neve Zohar gas station at junction of roads 90 and 31; 7 days a week but book a day ahead.

Transport
Jerusalem buses all stop at Ein Boqeq: there are several stops in the main tourist centre and one at the southern beach. For onward public transport see page 119 (though you will have to add or subtract 10 mins or so, and bear in mind that some services stop at Ein Gedi Beach for a break).

Car hire
Hertz, in the Solarium, T08-6584530/054-3999020.
Sunair, T054-5652883, sunairmzd@walla. co.il. Glider flights over Ein Gedi and Masada. Also do camel treks and abseiling.

Sodom (Sedom) Region

Tradition holds that this is the cursed land of Sodom and Gomorrah, though many Israelis will tell you that the night-spots of Tel Aviv or Eilat are the modern Sodom and Gomorrah. The region is one of austere, terrifying beauty; a fitting scene for where "the Lord rained upon Sodom and upon Gomorrah brimstone and fire … and he overthrew those cities, and all the plain, and all the inhabitants of the cities, and that which grew upon the ground" (Genesis 19:24-25).

Arriving in the Sodom (Sedom) Region
Geography The dominant geographical features are the salt flats of the Dead Sea to the east, with their bizarre sculptured forms, and the Mt Sodom range to the west. This range, 11 km long but just 2 km wide, is the lowest mountain range in the world and is largely composed of salt. The highest point is 240 m above the Dead Sea, but still -200 m below sea level. The range is underlain by a salt rock layer 2750 m deep. Though annual rainfall is less than 50 mm, water leaking into the fissures between the harder rock and the salt rock has formed vertical chimneys and lateral caves and tunnels. Other formations formed by the erosive action of water resemble pillars and statues, including the famous Lot's wife (see Genesis 19:26). The cliff face lining this section of Route 90 is riddled with cave complexes, the soft limestone cliffs carved by water action into spectacular, swirling shapes. Unfortunately, **Salt (or Sedom) Cave** and the **Flour Cave** (so named because of the flour-like residue that lines the canyons) have both been deemed unsafe, and neither is accessible to tourists. Check with locals in case this situation changes, though it is unlikely to.

Dead Sea Works
This is an unattractive industrial complex (you can't miss it) that is vital to the economic needs of Israel. The original Dead Sea Works were founded on the northern shore in 1930, with those here being built four years later.

Ne'ot HaKikar and Ein Tamar

Nestled on the Jordanian border, this agricultural moshav (village) makes an excellent alternative base for exploring the Dead Sea and eastern Negev regions. Surrounded by date palms and with views of the Edom Mountains to the east, there are accommodation options for a range of budgets and easy-to-access hiking and biking routes along local wadis. A supremely friendly place: ask a local to reveal the way to the hidden spring – a freshwater pool perfect for a dip on (the many) hot days. A map of Ne'ot HaKikar and adjacent Ein Tamar is available from the tourist information centre in Ein Boqeq.

Ne'ot Hakikar & Ein Tamar listings

For hotel and restaurant price codes and other relevant information, see pages 12-16.

Where to stay

$$$ Villa Villekulla, T08-6572759/052-8666062, barakhorwitz@gmail.com. Named after Pippi Longstocking's house, this place is perfect for a small group of friends or families. Both bedrooms have TV, 2 bathrooms, fully functioning kitchen, sofa-bed in living room, futon on veranda, space to throw down mattresses, games and books (Hebrew and English). Shady garden is the big attraction, with BBQ, passion fruit vines dangling overhead, lovely night lamps, and decking area with built-in jacuzzi. The owner, Barak, provides jeep tours (see below) and is good for info on hikes in the area.

$$$-$$ Belfer's Dead Sea Cabins, T08-6555104/052-5450970, michalbelfer@gmail.com. 3 cute wood cabins with views from the porch to the mountains of Jordan. The mezzanine accessed by a ladder sleeps 3, plus double bedroom, comfy sitting area, kitchenette, nice bathroom with jacuzzi, TV, Wi-Fi, light-coloured wood throughout. Each has picnic table and BBQ. Help yourself to herbs from the garden or tomatoes from the fields. Free bikes, jeep tours and guided walks available. A quality place run by lovely people. Small price rise at weekends.

$$-$ Shkedi's Camp Lodge, T052-2317371. www.shkedig.com, shkedi.camplodge@gmail.com. 2 quirky a/c private huts with wooden and rock walls, coloured glass windows and bamboo ceilings (no en suite). Dormitories offered in greenhouse-shaped tents are cheery and cosy (old-fashioned stoves for winter nights, fans in summer); sleep up to 15 (or take as 'private' for a reasonable price). Large tent sleeps up to 70, curtain split area. Bring your own sleeping bag, or borrow one of theirs. Mattresses are exceedingly comfy whichever accommodation you choose. Constant background of cool music, busy with Israeli families at weekends (expect to be invited to share *poikas* around the campfire). Shared kitchen, BBQs, excellent showers, communal area with bar, warm and welcoming hosts who make a stay very memorable. Couple of bikes for guests' use, Wi-Fi throughout. Jeep tours. Collection from bus stop provided. Recommended.

Restaurants

$$ Inbar Bakikar, T057-7743418. Close by the swimming pool, 'Inbar on the Square' is open all year round for breakfast (55NIS), lunch and dinner (80-100NIS) and snacks. Tunisian-style food, both veg and non-veg. Ayala is a lovely host. Book in advance for dinner/breakfast.

$$ Yossi's Place, T052-8911658. Sun-Thu 1400-2000 (opens Sat if bookings). Look for the coloured lights outside. Inside it's no frills and bamboo-lined walls. All about home-cooked food that is hearty and high quality; mainly meat (enormous steaks, mini-burger-style kebabs recommended) though vegetarians will enjoy the wonderful entrée salads (hot herzilim baladi – seared eggplant with tahina), hummus and quiche. Everything, down to the pickles, is home-made. Mains 65-90NIS, alcohol served.

$$-$ Pnina's Restaurant-Café, T08-6555107. Sun-Thu 1000-1600, Fri 1000-1430. Resident of the moshav since it began, Pnina serves breakfasts (40NIS), and snacks (good omelette and schnitzel sandwiches) in her garden. Her husband grills the fresh fish that he farms (about 70NIS) for lunch. Best to call in advance.

Festivals

Every year during the holiday of Sukkot (Sep/Oct) the HaTamar Festival is held in the desert for 5 days amid spectacular scenery, with free events and Israeli musicians. Contact the Tourist Information Centre in Ein Boqeq for more details.

Shopping

Estee's Pottery, T08-6552828/052-8991147, esteeuzi@zahav.net.il, www.deadseaceramics.co.il. Workshop/gallery in a charming setting, Estee's work is inspired by the agriculture of the moshav – her ceramic peppers and pumpkins are iconic. She also gives workshops: you can fire your own glaze designs using pit-fire or Raku (Japanese) techniques. Daily 1000-1700, but call in advance. Estee's husband Uzi (T052-8991146, www.cycle-inn.com) rents out mountain bikes and provides information on routes in the desert valleys. Groups can stay at the well-equipped **Cycle Inn**.

JoJo, Ein Tamar, T08-6551543/052-2964677, www.jojo-art.com. You may have noticed the colourful metal sculptures adorning Ein Boqeq and the region. They all stem from the funky gallery of Moroccan-born artist JoJo. He specializes in huge slender vases and peculiarly comfortable chairs, though there are also some smaller and more portable items for sale. His wife, Dganit, does lively acrylic paintings on wood in the vein of Jackson Pollock. To find JoJo, turn left from the roundabout at the entrance to the moshav and follow the vases to the warehouse-like workshop. Also has a gallery in Tel Aviv.

What to do
Agricultural tours

Despite the highly saline soil, this little corner of Israel is a major exporter of peppers, melons, dates, etc to Europe and beyond. Interestingly, Thai employees on the farms now outnumber the local community by almost 2 to 1. An agricultural tour of the moshav gives a valuable and fascinating insight into the technological innovations and sheer perseverance involved. Arrange a tour through Shkedi's Camp, 200NIS for 1½ hrs.

Cycling

See **Estee's Pottery**, above.

Jeep tours

Barak Horwitz, T052-8666062, barak horwitz@gmail.com. Barak can answer questions on pretty much any topic, and is a sure source of information about the desert region, its plants, economics and history. Jeep tours in any direction (but east!) can range from 2 hrs to 2 days. 800NIS for 8 people 2 hrs, 4 hrs 1200NIS, 6-7 hrs 1500NIS, day/night 2000NIS (camping gear provided, a/c vehicle).

Shkedi's Desert Tours (see Camp Lodge, above, for contact). Another trustworthy and experienced guide to the desert, a/c jeep (can be the best of activities on a scorching day), competitive prices.

Swimming

The moshav has a partially shaded swimming pool, open Apr-Sep, and is a glorious respite on a summer's day, adults 30NIS, children 15NIS.

Transport

The Jerusalem-Eilat bus 444 stops at Kikar Sodom junction on Road 90, 4 daily in each direction (restricted service Fri/Sat). For **Tel Aviv**, buses 393 and 394 leave from Arava junction (at least 10 daily). The bus to **Eilat** can be especially busy: it's a good idea to phone and book a seat in advance.

Contents

Footnotes

Index

Titles available in the Footprint *Focus* range

Latin America	UK RRP	US RRP
Bahia & Salvador	£7.99	$11.95
Brazilian Amazon	£7.99	$11.95
Brazilian Pantanal	£6.99	$9.95
Buenos Aires & Pampas	£7.99	$11.95
Cartagena & Caribbean Coast	£7.99	$11.95
Costa Rica	£8.99	$12.95
Cuzco, La Paz & Lake Titicaca	£8.99	$12.95
El Salvador	£5.99	$8.95
Guadalajara & Pacific Coast	£6.99	$9.95
Guatemala	£8.99	$12.95
Guyana, Guyane & Suriname	£5.99	$8.95
Havana	£6.99	$9.95
Honduras	£7.99	$11.95
Nicaragua	£7.99	$11.95
Northeast Argentina & Uruguay	£8.99	$12.95
Paraguay	£5.99	$8.95
Quito & Galápagos Islands	£7.99	$11.95
Recife & Northeast Brazil	£7.99	$11.95
Rio de Janeiro	£8.99	$12.95
São Paulo	£5.99	$8.95
Uruguay	£6.99	$9.95
Venezuela	£8.99	$12.95
Yucatán Peninsula	£6.99	$9.95

Asia	UK RRP	US RRP
Angkor Wat	£5.99	$8.95
Bali & Lombok	£8.99	$12.95
Chennai & Tamil Nadu	£8.99	$12.95
Chiang Mai & Northern Thailand	£7.99	$11.95
Goa	£6.99	$9.95
Gulf of Thailand	£8.99	$12.95
Hanoi & Northern Vietnam	£8.99	$12.95
Ho Chi Minh City & Mekong Delta	£7.99	$11.95
Java	£7.99	$11.95
Kerala	£7.99	$11.95
Kolkata & West Bengal	£5.99	$8.95
Mumbai & Gujarat	£8.99	$12.95

Africa & Middle East	UK RRP	US RRP
Beirut	£6.99	$9.95
Cairo & Nile Delta	£8.99	$12.95
Damascus	£5.99	$8.95
Durban & KwaZulu Natal	£8.99	$12.95
Fès & Northern Morocco	£8.99	$12.95
Jerusalem	£8.99	$12.95
Johannesburg & Kruger National Park	£7.99	$11.95
Kenya's Beaches	£8.99	$12.95
Kilimanjaro & Northern Tanzania	£8.99	$12.95
Luxor to Aswan	£8.99	$12.95
Nairobi & Rift Valley	£7.99	$11.95
Red Sea & Sinai	£7.99	$11.95
Zanzibar & Pemba	£7.99	$11.95

Europe	UK RRP	US RRP
Bilbao & Basque Region	£6.99	$9.95
Brittany West Coast	£7.99	$11.95
Cádiz & Costa de la Luz	£6.99	$9.95
Granada & Sierra Nevada	£6.99	$9.95
Languedoc: Carcassonne to Montpellier	£7.99	$11.95
Málaga	£5.99	$8.95
Marseille & Western Provence	£7.99	$11.95
Orkney & Shetland Islands	£5.99	$8.95
Santander & Picos de Europa	£7.99	$11.95
Sardinia: Alghero & the North	£7.99	$11.95
Sardinia: Cagliari & the South	£7.99	$11.95
Seville	£5.99	$8.95
Sicily: Palermo & the Northwest	£7.99	$11.95
Sicily: Catania & the Southeast	£7.99	$11.95
Siena & Southern Tuscany	£7.99	$11.95
Sorrento, Capri & Amalfi Coast	£6.99	$9.95
Skye & Outer Hebrides	£6.99	$9.95
Verona & Lake Garda	£7.99	$11.95

North America	UK RRP	US RRP
Vancouver & Rockies	£8.99	$12.95

Australasia	UK RRP	US RRP
Brisbane & Queensland	£8.99	$12.95
Perth	£7.99	$11.95

For the latest books, e-books and a wealth of travel information, visit us at: www.footprinttravelguides.com.

Join us on facebook for the latest travel news, product releases, offers and amazing competitions: www.facebook.com/footprintbooks.